'This book makes an original contribution to a n
A must read for anyone interested in educationa
and equity.'

Dr Khalwant Bhopal, Reader in Education, University of Southampton

'This is a timely and impressively well-researched and informed
contribution to the much needed debate and action to secure equality in
education for the most marginalized communities in Europe. It should be
a welcome reminder to all those concerned with ensuring that all children
have equal access to quality inclusive education, including Gypsy, Roma
and Traveller children.'

**Arthur R. Ivatts OBE, International Consultant on Inclusive Education
and Human Rights concerned mainly with Roma, Gypsy and Traveller
communities in Europe**

Travellers and Home Education

IOEPress Trentham Books

Travellers and Home Education
Safe spaces and inequality

Kate D'Arcy

A Trentham Book
Institute of Education Press

First published in 2014 by the Institute of Education, University of London,
20 Bedford Way, London WC1H 0AL
www.ioe.ac.uk/ioepress

British Library Cataloguing in Publication Data:
A catalogue record for this publication is available from the British Library

ISBNs
978-1-85856-554-5 (paperback)
978-1-85856-625-2 (PDF eBook)
978-1-85856-626-9 (ePub eBook)
978-1-85856-627-6 (Kindle eBook)

Every effort has been made to trace copyright holders and to obtain their permission for the use of copyright material. The publisher apologizes for any errors or omissions and would be grateful if notified of any corrections that should be incorporated in future reprints or editions of this book.

The opinions expressed in this publication are those of the author and do not necessarily reflect the views of the Institute of Education, University of London.

Typeset by Quadrant Infotech (India) Pvt Ltd
Printed by CPI Group (UK) Ltd, Croydon CR0 4YY

Contents

Why Gypsies and other Travellers home educate

Educational spaces and inequality

The links between Gypsies, Travellers, home education and educational inequality may not be immediately obvious. Gypsies and Travellers are seldom thought of as home educators at all (Monk, 2009). Still, Gypsy and Traveller communities form a distinctive and ever-growing group of home educators in England and it has been estimated that, in some local authorities, up to one-third of all home-educated children are Gypsy or other Traveller children (Ivatts, 2006).

My knowledge of Travellers' use of home education stems from my previous role as a practitioner working with Traveller communities. I observed the difficulties Gypsy and Traveller children experienced in school and the growing numbers of Traveller families who were opting for home education, particularly at the secondary school phase. Yet I found that there was little research on home education in the UK and even less on Gypsies' and Travellers' experiences of this educational alternative. It thus seemed vitally important to explore Gypsies' and Traveller's reasons for home educating their children and to listen to their experiences and perceptions of home education.

I undertook my own research into this area, investigating the reasons for home education among 11 Romany Gypsy and Showman families. Racism, bullying and discrimination in school were commonly cited reasons for the uptake of elective home education (EHE): these Traveller families chose home education as a safe educational space. This research revealed how the British education system does not facilitate the opportunities that Gypsy and other Traveller families desire for their children's success. It revealed unequal educational provision and processes within the educational spaces studied (mainstream school and EHE). Widespread racism still denies equitable educational opportunities to many Traveller children. This book documents the rarely heard accounts of a sample of Gypsy and other Traveller families to inform current understandings of racism, school and home education.

Kate D'Arcy

Acknowledgements

The content of the book is based upon my doctoral research and I am very grateful to all those who agreed to participate in this research project. I am especially grateful to all the Traveller families who participated, and hope that documenting their voices will result in better insights and understandings about education and inequality.

I want to thank Gillian Klein, my editor, who actively supported my book proposal and the writing process from start to finish. Finally, I would like to thank Ken Marks, who inspired my initial research ideas, Arthur Ivatts and Chris Derrington, and my family and friends for their support and faith in my work.

About the author

Kate D'Arcy trained as a primary teacher and then as a youth and community worker. She has worked in education for many years, mainly on the margins, supporting vulnerable and often disengaged young people. As a practitioner in a Traveller Education Service she was directly engaged in improving educational access and achievement for Gypsy, Roma and Traveller pupils and their families. She now continues her pursuit of social justice by teaching her students in Higher Education about inclusion and exclusion in education. Her research interests are centred on Gypsy, Roma and Traveller communities' educational positions, on race equality and education, on practitioner-led research and on digital technologies and learning. Having observed at first hand the inequalities that Traveller children and their families experience in education and wider society, she is committed to anti-discriminatory practice and actively promotes inclusion, equality and diversity in her work. She hopes with this book to raise awareness of ongoing inequalities for Gypsies and Travellers and to mobilize action.

Chapter 1

Home education and educational inequality

Sherry-Anne is an only child. Diagnosed with special educational needs (SEN) early on at primary school, she attended speech therapy outside of school and received teacher assistant support in the classroom. She is calm and quiet and has had lots of friends at primary school, both Travellers and non-Travellers. Sherry-Anne completes primary school but does not move up to secondary school; Mum and Dad are unsure about sending her there. They fill out the forms for elective home education (EHE).

But Mum is worried. She sees the Traveller Education Service (TES) worker out and about and talks to her. She says she can't find a tutor for Sherry-Anne, as she does not know anyone who can teach her. The EHE service cannot give her a list of approved tutors and other families won't give her any contacts for their tutors. Because Sherry-Anne is now home educated she no longer gets speech therapy. Mum thinks that without this support and a tutor she will stop making the good progress she made at primary school – she will stop learning. Mum can't read or write. Dad can, a bit: he spends time with Sherry-Anne in the evenings, reading books.

Mum, then, wants to give secondary school a try. Sherry-Anne says she will go. They all visit the school and talk to the head of Year Seven. Sherry-Anne is given a date to start. But Sherry-Anne does not go. Dad phones the school just before she is due to start, telling them 'We are moving to Birmingham'. The TES worker who has been supporting the family knows this is not true. She goes to talk to them and finds that they are not moving anywhere. But Dad is really worried about sending Sherry-Anne to school. It is too big; she might not tell them if she gets bullied.

Sherry-Anne is not the girl's real name, but this is a common story – one that will be familiar to professionals working with Traveller families and to those supporting Gypsy and Traveller children in accessing mainstream education. Sherry-Anne does not go to secondary school, though Mum still wants her to. Eventually the family find someone who can do some schoolwork with her for an hour a week to support her home education. That is all the family can afford.

In England, home education is a legal educational alternative to school, but little is known about those who home educate and the methods they use. The official term for this type of education is elective home education (EHE). This book provides information about EHE generally. It pays particular attention to Travellers' perspectives and experiences of EHE and to educational inequalities within school and home education. Three questions are considered:

- Why do Gypsies and other Traveller families choose home education?
- What are Gypsies and Travellers' experiences and perceptions of home education?
- What equality issues are evident in Gypsy and other Traveller families' use of home education?

Introduction

Though most families in England today send their children to mainstream schools, parents can legally choose to educate their children at home. Home education is not new: parents have taught their own children throughout recorded history (Petrie, 2001). Traditionally, home education has been popular particularly with affluent families, who can forego earnings and still be able to provide for their child's education (Lubienski, 2003). Gabb (2004) tells us that it was the custom of kings and queens to have their children home educated. For some other families home education has been a necessity: geographically isolated families, such as those living in remote areas of Australia, often had no choice but to home educate.

Home education, then, was common for many children before school systems were established and, even after the evolution of school-based education, remains a serious alternative to institutional, compulsory schooling. Still, a lack of research and accurate data on home education in England makes it difficult to establish the number of children involved. Current EHE guidance does not require parents or carers who are home educating their children to make themselves known to their local authority (LA). There are therefore no national statistics that give the exact number of EHE children in England. Estimated numbers, however, suggest that the number of home-educated children is growing: the most recent estimate gauged the total number to exceed 80,000 (Badman, 2009).

It is also difficult to gather a comprehensive picture of the circumstances and content of home education. For this reason, perhaps, home education and home educators are often looked upon as different, deviant and strange. LA officers and teachers are often astonished that parents feel that they can provide their children with an education of the same standard as school (Webb, 2010). Even though school attendance is a more recent development than home education, it is schooling that is today seen as necessary, even essential, for healthy child development (Monk, 2004). Yet we know that many children, including Gypsy and Traveller, experience problems at school. This is apparent when we consider the achievement and attendance of certain groups of children. Gypsy and Traveller children have experienced long-term underachievement in mainstream school in England (Tyler, 2005). Today, they remain the groups with the lowest rates of attendance and of academic attainment (Levinson, 2013). For Gypsy and Traveller children, mainstream schooling systems are not necessarily supportive of their welfare and development; I argue that it is for this reason that many families resort to home education.

Arthur Ivatts (2006) considered the specific situations affecting Gypsies, Travellers and home education. He undertook a small study spanning 23 LAs in England and identified a total of 2,989 children across them who were officially registered for EHE. Approximately one-third of these children (1,023) were Gypsies and Travellers. His figures reinforced the idea that a considerable number of parents, including Traveller parents, are home educating. It is important to highlight that this is only the number of registered children; many more children may be participating in EHE but are not registered as such.

In a time when mainstream education and the achievement of pupils are regularly scrutinized, it is also perhaps surprising that the area of EHE has until recently attracted little attention. This began to change in 2009 when the Labour Government requested a review into this educational alternative; the details and outcomes of this review are explained in Chapter 3.

This book focuses upon the legal educational spaces of state school and home education. Other legal educational alternatives, such as Pupil Referral Units and private education, are not considered. Beyond these settings, there are also children who are missing from education altogether – these are children who are not registered in any provision (including for

EHE), for any of a number of reasons. This cohort of missing children includes significant numbers of Traveller children. Unfortunately there is too little space in this book to explore the particular issues of missing children. It is certainly an area of interest I hope to explore in the future, not least as Ofsted (1999; 2003) estimated that 12,000 Traveller pupils of secondary age were not registered in any school.

There are various ways for children to be educated, including formal and informal options. Figure 1.1 illustrates the various educational arrangements available to and used by Gypsy and other Traveller families in the LA I studied. From here on, I refer to this LA as Saltfield – a pseudonym to protect the identities of the families who took part in my research. The picture of educational options for children will vary between LAs. This book concentrates on the experiences and perceptions of those Gypsy and Traveller families in Saltfield who are registered as home educating.

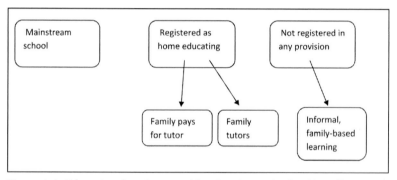

Figure 1.1: Educational options used by Gypsies and other Traveller families in Saltfield

The home educating families I talked to in Saltfield had specific social characteristics. Nine families were Romany Gypsies and two were Showmen. For more information about Traveller groups and their backgrounds see Chapter 2. The families I interviewed all lived in trailers on public and private sites across the LA, but their financial circumstances varied widely. The book draws also on interviews with the two main professionals responsible for EHE in Saltfield, from whom I gathered information on local EHE systems and practices. It is important to point out that the circumstances in my sample families may not typify the uptake of EHE by Gypsies and Travellers nationally.

A note on terminology

At this stage it is important to clarify some of the key terms used in this book and my reasons for using them.

Gypsies and other Travellers

'Traveller' is a commonly accepted term that covers a range of identifiable ethnic groups, the largest being Romany Gypsies, Roma and Irish Travellers. The term Traveller is also sometimes extended to include Occupational Travellers, the most significant group being the Fairground or Showman community. New Age Travellers, a more recent occupational travelling group, are not the focus of this book. Here I concentrate on Romany Gypsies and Showmen, and therefore refer in the text to Gypsies and other Travelling communities. In some cases this is abbreviated for convenience to Gypsies and Travellers, and I hope this does not cause any offence to Showmen.

Travellers from the Romany Gypsy and Irish groupings have been living in Britain since the fifteenth century. They maintain a strong sense of cultural identity. The exact numbers of Gypsies and Travellers in England is unknown, since these groups were not enumerated in the national census until 2011. In 2006 it was estimated that there were approximately 300,000 Romany Gypsies in Britain (CRE, 2006).

Clark (2006) estimated the much smaller Showman population to number between 21,000 and 25,000 people. Clark notes the strong sense among the Showmen of themselves as a community with its own culture and heritage. The nomadic traditions of this particular community date back to pre-Norman times (Showmen's Guild of Great Britain, 1987). The modern community has important roots in the Victorian era, with the arrival of steam-powered rides and other fairground attractions. From quite early on this community organized a national structure in the form of a Guild, which further cemented their distinctiveness:

> The formation of the United Kingdom Van Dwellers' Association in 1889 was the most decisive and important event in the history of travelling showpeople as a community … In 1917 the Showmen's Guild of Great Britain, as it became known, was recognised as the trade association of the travelling funfair business and acquired the right to stand as representatives for the business at both local and national levels, a position it still occupies to this day.
>
> (National Fairground Archive, 2012)

Whether a person is Gypsy, Roma or Traveller is a matter of self-ascription; the terms do not exclude those who live in houses. Ethnic or cultural identity is not lost when members of Traveller groups settle, but continues and adapts to new circumstances. Gypsies and Travellers live in a mixture of trailers, mobile homes and permanent housing (D'Arcy, 2011).

Romany Gypsies, Travellers of Irish heritage and Showman families are distinctive communities, but all attract a common pattern of hostility and prejudice. This seems to have developed because of their nomadic traditions (Kiddle, 1999; Danaher, 1995, 2001). Society has attached a derogatory label to Traveller communities based upon their perceived difference (Thompson, 2011). Racism and discrimination against Gypsies and Travellers has a long history and remains a pressing issue for all Traveller communities today.

Race, culture, equality and discrimination

Gillborn (1995) has suggested that it is *culture*, not just colour, that is increasingly the focal point of racist discrimination. It seems that the more a particular culture deviates from the assumed (white, middle class, Christian) norm, the higher the chance that it is excluded (Lander, 2011). In this book the term *racism* will be used to describe deliberate acts of prejudice. I focus particularly on the less obvious forms of racism that operate through a language of culture difference (Gillborn and Youdell, 2000). Travellers' cultural differences are used to portray them as undeserving, and this challenges any development educational improvement, social cohesion and justice.

There are many meanings for *equality*. In the literal sense, equality means sameness (Thompson, 2011). This meaning can be unhelpful, as politicians and policies might refer to equality when they mean uniformity (Gillborn, 1995). Promoting equality is not about offering the same, and the drive for equal opportunities is not simply about ensuring that opportunities are there for everyone. It should be about ensuring everyone can access those opportunities (Knowles, 2011) and achieve equitable outcomes. The notion of equality within this book entails treating people fairly notwithstanding their difference (Thompson, 2011). This is especially important when talking about Gypsies and Travellers. As Liegeois reminds us, 'policies towards Gypsies and Travellers have always constituted, in one form or another, a negation of the people and their culture' (Liegeois, 1998: 36).

Various forms of *discrimination* continue to have marked effects on the acceptance and inclusion of Gypsies and other Traveller children into mainstream schooling, especially at secondary level. This was apparent in Saltfield, where many Gypsy and Traveller families were found to be using EHE as an alternative to school. Actually, they were using it as an escape route from school; this finding is discussed throughout the book.

EHE and educational inequality

Although there is a good deal of literature and research on the difficulties Gypsy and Traveller children experience in school, there is little research about their experiences of EHE. As Gypsies and Travellers are a distinctive and ever-growing group of home educators, this exploration of their reasons for taking up EHE and their experiences and perceptions of EHE is important. This book documents Gypsies' and Travellers' personal views of EHE in Saltfield. Where much research has relied only on the stories told by professionals, here Travellers' voices are placed centre stage. This is because some professionals have criticized Gypsy and Traveller parents' ability to provide their children with a suitable education (Ivatts, 2006). I seek to challenge these suggestions by documenting Gypsies' and other Travellers' own stories.

The vast majority of Gypsy and Traveller children in England do attend primary education, yet the amount of dropouts during secondary transition and at secondary school is high. Tracking an entire cohort of Traveller children between 2003 and 2008 revealed that although 80 per cent of Gypsy and Traveller pupils transferred to secondary school, only 51 per cent were still attending by Year 11, the final year (Wilkin *et al.*, 2010: 70). Not all Traveller children who drop out of mainstream education take up EHE. Many children are simply not registered in any provision, although relatives may be providing informal, family-based learning (see Figure 1.1).

Nevertheless, studying those who have registered for EHE highlights emerging issues of educational inequality. Research into EHE, Gypsies and Travellers (Ivatts, 2006) revealed that Gypsy and Traveller parents are often manoeuvred into EHE at secondary school level due to fear of cultural erosion, a perception that the school curriculum lacks relevance, and fear of racist and other bullying (Ivatts, 2006: 4). This suggests that the move to EHE is linked to inequality issues in school. Worryingly, there is also evidence that the numbers of Gypsy and Traveller families taking up EHE is rising (Ivatts, 2006).

When Badman (2009) reviewed EHE systems in England he recognized that there were many families (not just Gypsies and Travellers) who chose home education by default rather than for positive reasons, and raised this as a concern. For all these reasons, and because Travellers' experiences of home education have not been well documented, research into this area is important.

As I listened to Gypsies' and other Travellers' own experiences I heard worrying tales about inequalities and injustices in school. My study became a critical one: I wanted to document the inequalities I was hearing about. My research therefore included a theoretical dimension that supported the understanding of inequality and discrimination. I drew upon Critical Race Theory (CRT) as a critical lens through which processes of racism and Othering, which normalize and validate Gypsy and Traveller children's educational inequalities, can be highlighted. CRT has been described as a useful approach towards anti-racist work (Gillborn, 2006) and its ideas and methods are discussed in Chapter 6. This book uses two specific CRT approaches, storytelling and counter-stories, to tell Gypsies' and Travellers' experiences of home education and school and to challenge negative assumptions about Travellers and education. The aim is to improve education and address inequalities.

In this book, I use my research findings to tell the story of EHE in a local authority I call Saltfield. I tell the story to raise awareness of continuing inequalities in school and EHE. I anticipate that this will improve understanding about the children who are placed at the margins of education. I hope this text will serve as a reminder that racism and discrimination remain very serious issues in Gypsy and other Travellers' educational access and achievement. The prevalent negative stereotyping of and discrimination against all Traveller communities needs to be stopped, and there needs to be a change in attitude and a willingness to act to address educational and social injustice. There is also an urgent need for more critical discussions about school and EHE, and to acknowledge and include Gypsies' and other Travellers' experiences and views of school and EHE in this dialogue. These matters are highlighted throughout this book.

How this book is organized

Chapter 2 outlines briefly the backgrounds of Gypsies and other Traveller groups. Chapter 3 looks at home education in England, drawing comparisons with Europe, the United States and Australia. I discuss the current guidance that underpins EHE practices in England, and the resulting complexities and challenges. Badman's review of the EHE system in England is outlined to present an up-to-date picture of the EHE context.

Although the book concentrates upon home education, the literature and my own research both highlight associated issues with school and the uptake of EHE. Chapter 4 considers Gypsies' and Travellers' experiences of mainstream school, the role of Traveller Education Services and different Traveller children's experiences of education in England. Educational practices within eastern Europe regarding Roma children are also discussed.

Chapter 5 takes a critical approach to the literature on home education and Gypsy and Traveller communities to highlight the overt and covert forms of racism and discrimination that perpetuate educational disadvantage and social exclusion. Dominant, negative discourses about Gypsies and Travellers prevail within mainstream literature. I counteract these with the specific research on Gypsies and Travellers and EHE that portray the reality. Interestingly, disproportionate numbers of children with special educational needs and those labelled as gifted and talented take up EHE; this chapter draws attention to the similarities in experiences of schooling between Gypsies and Travellers and other groups of children who are seen as Others.

Chapter 6 focuses on the application of theory to research, and specifically on how Critical Race Theory applies to Gypsies, Travellers and home education. I propose that Critical Race Theory is an appropriate and useful premise to highlight racism within education as it places the experiences of those who are marginalized at centre stage, revealing the racist treatment of the Other and the complexities and challenges in combating racism.

Chapter 7 considers the ethical and practical considerations in undertaking research with marginalized groups. Although this chapter concentrates on Gypsies and other Travellers, the ideas and suggestions regarding respectful, ethical approaches can be applied to all those we research, and can inform our working practices and daily lives.

Chapter 8 documents Gypsies' and Travellers' experiences and practices of EHE and school. It concentrates on their own voices and their reasons for choosing home education as well as their experiences and perceptions of school and EHE.

Chapter 9 develops the narrative element of this book by providing three in-depth vignettes from Traveller families' stories of EHE. It presents the stories verbatim and provides readers with a real feel for different Travellers' situated realities. This presentation of Gypsies and Travellers' own words follows the Critical Race Theory principle of asserting the voices of the marginalized.

Throughout this book I highlight the challenges and complexities of the current EHE system in England. Chapter 10 offers as evidence a snapshot of Saltfield's EHE systems. This chapter draws on interviews with EHE professionals in Saltfield. It documents their views on suitable educational provision and draws on Badman's review of EHE. The motives they attribute to local families (including Gypsies and Travellers) for taking up EHE are also discussed.

Chapter 11 documents Romany Gypsy and Showman families' reasons for taking up EHE. Families always had more than one reason for opting for EHE; here they were associated with problems in school, especially at secondary level. This chapter sheds more light on their experiences and problems within school and indicates how EHE provides a safe space for many Gypsy and Traveller families. In the conclusion I return to answer the three specific questions regarding Gypsies, Travellers and EHE that were posed at the start of this chapter.

In Chapter 12, I summarize the key issues regarding racism, inequality and education for Gypsy and Traveller children and conclude with recommendations about ways of working towards equal educational opportunities and the social inclusion of Gypsies and other Travellers.

Chapter 2

Gypsies and other Traveller groups

Background information

The Romany people

It is thought that the ancestors of most Traveller groups who live in England, Ireland and the rest of Europe today migrated from Northern India about 1,000 years ago. Romany people, with their dark hair and skin, were referred to as Egyptians (shortened to 'Gypsies') because of a popular misconception that they came from Egypt.

There has always been prejudice against Gypsies and Travellers and they have been subject to discrimination in various forms. Romanies in Spain and Russia were kept as slaves. In what is now Romania, the Roma were forbidden to speak their language and worked as field or house slaves. After they were freed in 1864, little was done to support their reintegration and inclusion into mainstream society (Quarmby, 2013). In the UK, Romanies could be executed simply for being Gypsies; many were banished to America.

Gypsies and Travellers originally moved around the country on foot, in light carts or on horseback, sleeping outdoors or in barns, but by the nineteenth century, English Gypsies were using bender tents (made out of hazel and canvas) for shelter. The first wooden horse-drawn wagons appeared around 1820, used by Showmen and Fairground people. Gypsies adopted these several years later and used the term 'Vardo' for their wagons. By 1940, Gypsies and other Travellers had started to use motor-drawn trailers and buy their own land in England for stopping-places.

Gypsies and Travellers often keep horses. When the First World War broke out horses were needed for the war effort and were taken from Gypsies and Travellers; only horses that were dappled or piebald were left behind. Such dappled horses are now associated with Gypsies and Travellers by the dominant culture, where such horses are much sought-after today, particularly in America.

The persecution of Gypsies reached new levels in Germany in the 1930s. Roma were identified as having incurable mental illnesses, and when the Nazis came to power Hitler decreed that Roma people were undeserving of life (Fidyk, 2013). Thousands of Gypsies and Travellers were murdered in the Holocaust.

Two stereotypical images of the Gypsy Traveller have prevailed (Kenrick and Clarke, 1999). First was the romanticized image of the 'real' Gypsy, who travelled around in a horse-drawn wagon selling homemade products; then came the demonized image of the 'dirty' Gypsy who is poor and who steals. Allowing this Gypsy to live in any area, the stereotype holds, will bring down house prices and fill the local schools. They will not pay taxes and will leave rubbish everywhere.

In reality, however, Gypsies and Travellers do pay taxes and rent when they live on council-run sites. Indeed they often pay more rent for a site pitch (a slab of concrete with a utility room on it and access to mains electricity) than many people do for their council houses. Neither are Gypsies offered the opportunity to buy those pitches at a discounted rate, as council tenants can buy their houses. All the Travelling communities prize cleanliness and have strong views and rituals to promote a spotless home environment. Traveller sites are often located in dangerous environments: beside railway tracks, landfill sites and busy motorways, and rubbish is often dumped there by non-Travellers. Difficult living conditions and experiences of discrimination make Traveller parents protective of the safety and well-being of their children. Gypsies and Travellers remain some of the most disadvantaged groups in society and experience ongoing issues with accommodation. They have very poor health and high rates of infant mortality: one in five mothers loses a child in childbirth or early infancy.

Gypsies in England and Wales[1]

- An estimated 300,000 Gypsies live in Britain, but figures are still inconsistent (CRE, 2006).
- Gypsy families generally speak Romani or Welsh Romani. The Romani language was first recorded in England in 1542 and has many English words; Romani is mixed with English and uses mostly English grammar.
- Popular Gypsy trades include horse or vehicle trading, landscape gardening and tarmacking, building, property speculation and demolition.
- Most Gypsies and Travellers travel in trailers (caravans) pulled by lorries or cars.
- Some families prefer to be called Travellers because the word Gypsy is so often used pejoratively.

- Some Romani words have been adopted into English slang, including 'holler' (shout), 'brazen' (impolite) and 'kushti' (nice/lovely).
- Many Welsh Gypsies are Christian.
- The Gypsies of England and Wales are recognized as a minority ethnic group and are protected under the Race Relations Act and the Equality Act 2010.

Showmen and Fairground people

- There are around 21,000–25,000 people of the Showman community in Britain.
- Showmen are of many ethnicities, including Romani from several countries. Nonetheless they are not a minority ethnic group by law.
- Their travelling season extends through most of the year. Though old age and youth are respected, every member of the family contributes to the jobs to be done.
- The trailers and wagons families live in are large, modern and generally immaculate.
- Most families have a winter base where they go to maintain their rides for the following year. Their homes are often on large yards or sites, which accommodate their rides and the lorries that transport them.
- Children may attend school in lots of different places while the family is travelling but will return in the winter to their base school, where they tend to be registered long-term.

Irish Travellers

- The exact number of Irish Travellers in Britain is unknown; estimates vary from 15,000 to 30,000.
- Music is an extremely important part of Irish Traveller culture. The most common instruments are the fiddle and the spoons, and tunes and songs are passed down through generations.
- It can be difficult for Irish Travellers to find work in Ireland because they encounter racism and prejudice. Nevertheless they make a significant contribution to the rural economy. Popular trades include landscape gardening and tarmacking.
- Boxing is a much enjoyed and celebrated sport among Irish Travellers. In 1996, boxer Francie Barrett was the first Traveller to represent the Irish Republic at the Olympic Games.
- Most families are Roman Catholics.

- Within their families Irish Travellers may speak Gammon, Cant or Shelta, which are all types of English. Some words may sounds similar to the Romani spoken by Gypsies.
- Irish Travellers are recognized as a minority ethnic group and are protected under the Race Relations Act.

Roma

- An estimated 12 million Roma live in Europe, with 90,000–120,000 estimated to be in the UK.
- Central and eastern Europeans, including the Roma, moved to western European states, including the UK, throughout the twentieth century (European Dialogue, 2009: 6). Before the recent accession of certain central and eastern European countries to the European Union (EU), Roma came to the UK mainly as asylum seekers, but few succeeded in claiming asylum and most were deported.
- Since the EU accession of several eastern European countries more Roma are coming to Europe. They move to England to find work and a decent education for their children and to escape from racism. These are the most common reasons they emphasize; they seek a country where their children can grow up without facing overwhelming prejudice on a daily basis (European Dialogue, 2009).
- Roma have established significant communities in many towns and cities of England, although there is little provision for them in some areas. The largest groups of Roma are Slovak, Czech and Romanian Roma communities.
- Many Roma in the UK live in poverty and can have similar difficulties accessing and achieving in education as Romany Gypsies, Irish Travellers and Showmen do.
- Consistently negative media coverage warning of an influx of Roma stokes xenophobia and perpetuates discrimination against Romany Gypsies.

Note

[1] The information given here on Gypsies, Showmen and Fairground people, and Travellers of Irish heritage is derived originally from the Saltfield LA Traveller Education Service.

Chapter 3

An alternative educational space

> The parent of every child of compulsory school age shall cause him to receive efficient full-time education suitable (a) to his age, ability and aptitude, and (b) to any special educational needs he may have, either by regular attendance at school or otherwise.
>
> (Education Act 1996, section 7)

This section in the Education Act 1996 provides the foundation for EHE guidance and practice in the UK. Internationally, all children have a right to an education (UNICEF, 2005). However, this right is interpreted differently across national educational policies and practices. Many countries allow home education, but some do not. In Germany, for example, home education is illegal and permitted only in rare, specific circumstances. Galloway (2003) suggests that because home education is an alternative to statutory provision it can symbolize a challenge to mainstream education systems. EHE policy and practice varies from country to country.

The Netherlands, Spain, Switzerland and France do not routinely permit home education, although they will consider individual circumstances. In France, if a family is permitted to home educate they must follow a specific curriculum and demonstrate particular skills (Taylor and Petrie, 2000). In Ireland, Australia and Sweden, parents must register their children; Swedish registrations must be renewed annually. In Finland and Norway, the LA will oversee all pupil progress, and they may ask home-educated children to undertake exams. In New Zealand, home-educated children must be registered in a school and should be taught as often and as well as in school (DCSF, 2009a; Badman, 2009). Badman (2009), having compared EHE approaches across nations, claims that England presently adopts the most liberal approach towards EHE.

Elective home education guidance

In England there is no EHE policy, although government guidance offers optional advice for LAs and parents. The most up-to-date guidance on EHE was published by the Department for Children, Schools and Families (DCSF) under the Labour Government in 2007. The subsequent administration's Department of Education (DfE) has recognized that these home education guidelines were produced by the previous administration and proposed that they will be reviewed in due course (DfE, 2011). To date, there is little evidence of this happening.

When considering the Education Act 1996 and existing EHE guidance it becomes apparent that three key phrases guide EHE: (1) 'or otherwise'; (2) 'full-time education'; and (3) 'suitable education'. These are explained in turn.

'Or otherwise'

In England, education is compulsory for children of statutory school age, but schooling is not. Parents have a duty to educate their children but there is no duty to send them to school. Parents can decide to teach them 'otherwise'.

Parents in England are not obliged to seek permission to home educate, nor legally required to tell the LA that they plan to home educate. If a child is registered at school, however, parents need to inform the school in writing if they intend to remove them and home educate. The school then reports the child's withdrawal to the LA. This data can provide LAs with some idea of how many children are home educated in their authority.

The situation for children who have a registered special educational need (SEN) is slightly different. The parents of these children must get consent to home educate from the LA. Gabb (2004) suggests that this exception is not intended to prevent home education; instead it ensures that the LA can maintain continuity in its provision for SEN. DCSF (2007) guidance also mentions Gypsies and other Traveller communities:

> LAs should have an understanding of, and be sensitive to, the distinct ethos and needs of Gypsy, Roma and Traveller communities. It is important that these families who are electively home educating are treated in the same way as any other families. Home education should not necessarily be regarded as less appropriate than in other communities.
>
> (DCSF, 2007:18)

Professional experience and the general literature on Gypsy and Traveller home educators indicate that this guidance is not always followed. I revisit this issue in Chapter 5.

Full-time education

Section 7 of the Education Act 1996 specifies that all children of statutory age should receive full-time education, but there is no legal definition of what this entails. Children in school normally attend for 22–25 hours a week, 38 weeks per year. However, this is not taken to determine a timetable for home education (DCSF, 2007). EHE can take place outside normal school hours or be made up by periods of one-to-one tuition; it is difficult to specify a number of teaching hours required. Home educators in England are not required to teach the National Curriculum, or to have a timetable or specific plan of learning activities. There is no requirement to teach formal lessons or mark completed work. There is no mention of assessment of children's progress against school-based age-specific standards. And finally, a parent or tutor for home-educated children needs no particular qualifications or training.

When parents decide to home educate they are, in essence, taking on full responsibility for their children's education. LAs are advised to offer advice and support on EHE if it is requested, but current EHE guidance is focused more upon what home educators do not need to do than on providing guidance on possible approaches. A feasible reason for this may be that home education is not simply another teaching approach. Webb (2010) suggests that it represents families adopting a different lifestyle and therefore that it is up to parents to decide how to proceed. Although parents have the overall responsibility for home education, LAs retain specific duties to ensure that all children receive a suitable education.

LA and parental responsibilities: a 'suitable' education?

The Education Act states that LAs must make sure that all children in their jurisdiction receive a suitable education, and must 'make arrangements to enable them to establish the identities, so far as it is possible to do so, of children in their area who are not receiving a suitable education' (DCSF, 2007). This is difficult for two reasons. First, there is no legal definition of a suitable education. Case law, with reference to a Jewish school, broadly described it as an education that:

> equips a child for life within the community of which he is a member, rather than the way of the country as a whole, so long as it does not foreclose the child's options in later years to adopt some other forms of life if he wishes to do so.
>
> (Juridical Review, 1985)

Case law suggests therefore that whatever type of education a child receives, it must not hinder that child's ability to be autonomous in later life. Those who object to the principle of home education object to it on this basis. For example, Lubienski (2003) says that EHE is problematic because it limits home-educated children's social networks and their long-term vocational choices.

Monk (2004) traced the wording of the current Education Act concerning EHE back to the Elementary Education Act 1870. He found that, in 1870, parents of children between the ages of 5 and 13 years were required to 'cause such children (unless there is some reasonable excuse) to attend school'. One 'reasonable excuse' would be if the child was 'under efficient instruction in some other manner' (Elementary Education Act 1870, section 74). Changes in society, education and employment since that time raise the question as to whether a legal wording based on the educational practices and social conditions of 1870 is still relevant or useful today.

The second factor making it difficult for LAs to establish which children are not receiving a suitable education is that they have no legal right to enter the homes of these, or any, children:

> LAs do not currently have any statutory duties to monitor EHE on a routine basis nor do they have the power to enter the homes or see children for the purpose of monitoring EHE provision.
>
> (DCSF, 2007)

Thus, LAs have to ask parents to inform them of their decision to home educate. Parents may be asked to agree to a visit by an EHE adviser, but can refuse to admit the adviser or even to inform the LA that they have decided to home educate. The LA can then only ask for alternative evidence that they are educating them suitably. One of the leading home education organizations in the UK, the charity Education Otherwise, suggests that:

> [p]arents are not legally required to give the LA access to their home or their child. Article 8 of the Human Rights Act 1998 requires respect for the privacy of home and family life, and it should be remembered that where parents choose not to allow access this does not of itself constitute a ground for concern about the education being provided. Parents may, for example, choose to meet a LA representative at a mutually convenient and neutral location, or they may choose not to meet at all.
>
> (Education Otherwise, 2005: 10)

Thus, for LAs, fulfilling their EHE duty is complex and difficult (Hopwood *et al.*, 2007). The vagueness of EHE legislation is also frustrating for some parents new to home educating. They are given no clear guidance on the nature or content of what they might teach at home. Arora (2006) consulted with home-educating families and confirmed that parents with children with SEN would have liked more contact with the LA on the subject of their child's educational progress. They also wanted access to resources and advice on specific educational problems. Thus, the research suggests that both professionals and home-educating families want clearer guidance and regulations for EHE.

To monitor whether EHE provision is suitable, it would be helpful to have a baseline against which to evaluate it, but judging a suitable education is difficult. Such judgement is subjective, as it depends on individual ideas of what the content and purpose of education should be. Moreover, within educational discourse the words 'education' and 'school' are often used interchangeably. Maybe this is why judgements regarding provision are often based upon mainstream school standards.

McIntyre-Bhatty (2007) proposes that educational evaluations based on established school practices and educational policies do not transfer easily to EHE, and can in fact be inapplicable, inappropriate and inaccurate. Still, it seems that most evaluations of EHE are derived from assessments of school-based education. Some European countries do specify standards for home education evaluation that relate closely to school-based education. This is not the case in England but, according to Kendall and Atkinson (2006), officers who conducted monitoring visits for EHE in England mainly had teaching backgrounds. This was indeed the case in Saltfield. In addition, there is a trend whereby reports, evaluations and studies of EHE in England tend to feature consultations with school professionals rather than with EHE experts; this matter is discussed in Chapter 5.

In summary, EHE legislation is vague and LAs lack the power to monitor provision. This has resulted in assorted EHE practices and procedures across LAs in England. Judging a suitable education is complex and contested: there is still no definition of what a suitable education might include. Clearly EHE, like mainstream schooling, encompasses children and families with widely differing needs. The concern is that it may be only confident and powerful individuals who benefit from the current system. While such individuals may have the resources to deliver home education and the influence to ensure that their voices are heard in debates on such matters, others may not. This is why it is important to look into the reasons why families whose children represent more marginalized and vulnerable groups home educate. Existing literature (Arora, 2006; Ivatts, 2006) suggests that it is because they are not having their needs met in school, yet these issues are rarely discussed or documented.

Reasons for home education

Families consider home education as an alternative to mainstream school for many reasons. DCSF (2007) guidance suggests that the main reasons parents in England home educate include: distance from (or difficulty of access to) school; religious or cultural beliefs; philosophical or ideological values; dissatisfaction with the education system; and, especially, bullying. EHE can be a short-term intervention for a particular reason, or a long-term response to dissatisfaction with mainstream education; it can also simply reflect parents' desire for a closer relationship with their children. The decision to home educate can consequently be part of a well-thought-out family plan, or a reaction to a crisis.

In 2002, Rothermel undertook a four-year study to explore the aims and practices of home educators. She investigated the possibility of classifying home educators according to their motives. Most attempts to categorize home educators draw on research in the USA, where there are large numbers of home educators. The most common motivator cited for US home-educating parents has been religion, as many US Christian families believe that it is the role of the family to educate their children (Van Galen, 1991; Webb, 2010). Van Galen (1991) suggested that the reasons why US parents home educate fall into two main categories: ideological and pedagogical. He hence categorized home-educating parents as either ideologues or pedagogues:

> Ideologues object to what is taught in schools and seek to strengthen intra-family relationships: they hold traditional, conservative and specific values; following a philosophy of Christian fundamentalism ... Pedagogues have educational reasons for homeschooling: school teaching is viewed as inept and the parents want to foster a broader interest in learning.
>
> (Rothermel, 2002: 77)

These categories are not applicable to the UK home education situation. Blacker (1981), in one of the earliest studies into home education, suggested three categories of home educators:

1. Competitors: formally qualified parents, competing with school to provide a better education.
2. Compensators: parents who agree with the philosophy of school but want to make up for a school's failure with their child.
3. Rebels: parents who have chosen an alternative lifestyle. They want individual freedom and reject social institutions.

These three categories may have provided some ideas about parents' motivation in the 1980s, but Rothermel (2003) maintains they are over-simplistic. Her research revealed diverse reasons for home educating and a more assorted cross-section of home educators than was the case over 30 years ago. Although it might be interesting to classify the main reasons why parents home educate, caution must be taken not to generalize all families. This is because there is relatively little data about home-educating families, and because the sample of families about whom we do have information does not necessarily represent all home educators' views.

Research (Arora, 2002, 2006; Rothermel, 2003; DCSF, 2007; Winstanley, 2009) shows that the reasons for which parents choose to home educate are diverse and can change. Home educators, like other families, are not a homogeneous group in any country. It is evident from this literature that parents have diverse motivations and approaches to home education. Therefore, Rothermel's (2003) suggestion to avoid generalized trends and taxonomies is sensible: generalizations can lead to misrepresentation of EHE. If vocal parents' opinions are generalized to the entire home-educating community, for example, then other, more marginalized groups' or individuals' needs will go unnoticed and unaddressed.

Although Rothermel warns against categorizing EHE families, others continue to do so. Webb (2010) makes two broad distinctions in his book on EHE in the UK: those who choose to undertake the education of their children as a positive decision and those who feel compelled to do so. These positive and negative categories are also referred to in DCSF (2007) guidance on EHE. Badman (2009) also classified reasons for home education as positive and negative in his *Review of Elective Home Education in England*. He highlighted particular concern about those families who elect for home education for negative reasons, or by default.

Kiddle (1999), a professional in the Traveller education field, also categorizes Gypsy and Traveller home educators. She initially categorizes Travellers' reasons for home educating thus: first, positive, well-planned intentions; secondly, more negative reasons, and thirdly, a less-informed route. She suggests that Gypsy or Traveller families in this third group are 'ignorant of the alternatives and base their decisions only on fears or hearsay about what goes on in schools' (Kiddle, 1999: 68). It is certainly true that fears about secondary school inform some Traveller parents' adoption of EHE. Still, I would classify these reasons as negative because they are found among parents who feel compelled to elect for EHE because of problems in school. Interestingly, Kiddle goes on to confirm this when she says that Travellers fear bullying and victimization, harassment by officials and a lack of understanding of their lifestyle and 'respect for their cultural values' in school (Kiddle, op. cit.: 69). Here, Travellers are choosing EHE for negative reasons. They are not rejecting formal education, but they are fearful for their children's welfare within it.

Even though the academic literature on EHE reflects a real interest in the reasons families elect for home education, this interest is not apparent in government guidance. The DCSF suggested that LAs' main concern should lie not with parents' reasons for home educating but in the suitability of parents' educational provision (DCSF, 2007: 3). There are differing views on this subject too. These are expanded in the next section, as they inform and direct understanding about EHE more generally.

Perspectives on home education

There are, generally speaking, three different views about the suitability of EHE:

- those who are critical of all home education;
- those who agree with the principle of EHE, but argue for better regulation of EHE systems;
- those who promote home education.

First, the critics: they include Brighouse (1997), Apple (2000), and Lubienski (2000; 2003). Such critics of EHE are worried about inequality, seeing EHE as preventing children from accessing important social and educational opportunities. One of the main concerns is the extent to which home education can offer the kinds of social contact and diversity found within school (Wyness, 2012). Lubienski dislikes EHE because it removes children from state schools. He feels that this disadvantages both the children removed and those left behind: losing children means a loss of diversity in a school. EHE is, to a great extent, an individualized route of education and this means that it can limit the development of wider social networks. Lubienski proposes that this is disadvantageous for society as a whole. He also argues that EHE limits children's choice and opportunities in later life: 'true choice is based on autonomy, where individuals are empowered to select from a range of alternatives' (Lubienski, 2003: 174). Brighouse (1997) disapproves of the total responsibility accorded to parents concerning home education. He thinks that granting parents unconditional rights regarding their children's education jeopardizes children's opportunities to become independent.

Second, there are those who agree with the principle of EHE but argue that it should be subject to better state guidelines and control.

Reich (2002) criticizes the manner in which home education is currently regulated. He argues that an element of formal teaching is needed as part of EHE, to balance the interests of the child, the parents and the state. Reich (2002) also states that educating is not the same as parenting. His view concerns children's rights. He feels that parents must share authority over the education of their children with the state and the child to ensure that children can access their right to a suitable education.

Finally, there are those who promote EHE. Ray (2000), who writes about American home education, argues that home education is driven by care and concern for children. He argues that home education does not harm the social capital of society, as home-educated children will ultimately serve their communities anyway. Among those who defend home education there are strong feelings about parental freedom and rights over their children's education. Home education associations in the US (for example, the Home School Legal Defense Association) and UK (Education Otherwise) vocally defend parental rights and choice in children's education: the rise in home education could thus be related to the increasing demand for parental choice in education. Carper and Tyler (2000) say that home education satisfies both parental and state interest, but the extent to which this is true depends on the country in question: some countries do not support home education, and others (like the UK) have trouble monitoring it because of LAs' limited powers. Thus, the issue of rights and interests is contested, and it is clear that not all countries are satisfied with EHE.

There is a debate between critics and supporters of EHE about the level of parental choice and power appropriate in children's education and futures. Brighouse (1997) proposes that education should be a collective responsibility, not down to parents alone, but something that society owes to each individual child. Reich (2002) reminds us that there are tripartite interests at stake in the education of children: the state, the parents and the child. There is evidence of the state's and parent's opinions on EHE, but children's own voices and influence regarding educational matters remains limited.

In recent years there has been a growing interest in children's rights within education. Article 12 of the 1989 United Nations Convention on the Rights of the Child (UNCRC) states that children should have a say in procedures that involve them (UNICEF, 2005). Recent educational developments on children's rights and welfare under Labour governments drew attention to EHE via the Every Child Matters agenda. The aim of this agenda was for every child, whatever their background or circumstances, to have the support they need to 'be healthy, stay safe, enjoy and achieve, make a positive contribution and achieve economic well-being' (Department for Education and Skills [DfES], 2004: 6). This agenda encouraged scrutiny of any policies or practices concerning children in order to ensure the development of their potential.

This political focus, combined with interest in the growing number of home-educated children and increasing concerns from LA children's services about the effectiveness of EHE systems, came to a head in 2008 with the death of a 7-year-old girl who was home educated (Webb, 2010). As a result, in January 2009, the Labour Government commissioned Graham Badman to assess the current system of home education. The process and outcomes of this review are now explained.

The Badman review of EHE in England

Early in 2009, Graham Badman undertook a review of English EHE systems to assess whether they enabled all children to receive a good education and stay safe and well (DCSF, 2010). Badman was to concentrate upon two main issues: first, the barriers to effectively carrying out LA safeguarding responsibilities; and second, whether LAs were providing the right support for home-educating families. The DCSF (2010) stated that its rationale for the review was based upon the commitment to ensure that systems for keeping children safe and ensuring they received a suitable education were as robust as possible. The accountability of government bodies was therefore an influencing factor in initiating and conducting this review.

Badman's review involved interviewing home-educating parents and their children as well as LA staff and home education groups. A call for evidence from the public via an online consultation received over 2,000 responses. In addition, questionnaires were sent out to those LAs judged to be providing the highest quality services; these achieved a 60 per cent response rate. The report was also informed by a literature review and a consideration of practice and legislation in other countries.

In June 2009, Badman produced his commissioned report. He suggested that current guidance was not sufficiently robust to protect the rights of all children. EHE guidance should be better defined and supported through improved access to services and facilities. Badman made a total of 28 recommendations. He proposed that a national registration scheme and new legislative powers for LAs should be introduced immediately so that LAs could establish the number of home-educated children in their jurisdictions and monitor EHE provision. LAs, he proposed, should have the right to access the dwellings of home-educated children to establish their safety and well-being. He also recommended better information sharing between LA services, especially about any substantiated concerns they might have about home-educating parents' ability to provide a suitable education. The DCSF should also make necessary legislative changes to allow LAs to refuse EHE registration on safeguarding grounds. Badman also suggested that the definition of 'suitable education' needed to be revised and improved to support the monitoring of EHE. These proposals would bring English EHE regulations into line with other countries' regulations.

The overall intention of Badman's 28 recommendations was to improve the EHE system, not to prevent EHE. Badman wanted to strike a balance between the rights of parents and children and the need for greater safety. His report and recommendations were initially accepted by the DCSF and made available for further public consultation until October 2009. During this time they received strong criticism from powerful (non-Traveller) home-educating groups, which coordinated a campaign to reject any changes to existing policy. This opposition to Badman's report was linked to concerns about the way in which the government and press associated home education with child abuse (Thomas and Pattison, 2010). The evidence of child abuse among home educators is very sparse indeed.

Badman's (2009) report also made clear that a better balance was needed between the rights of the parent and the rights of the child. This argument prompted anxiety from Education Otherwise, a UK home education group, who felt that the recommendations would act to replace parental rights with responsibilities defined by the state. Section 7 of the Education Act 1996 in fact already states that it is a parent's duty to ensure their child receives a suitable education, but does not state that the child's education is a parental right. Monk (2009) suggests that the notion of rights in education, as in domestic law, should not envisage 'unfettered autonomy for parents but a relationship between parents, children and the state' (p. 160). I argue that Badman's attempt to redress the balance of rights between child and parent within EHE should, then, be seen as a positive and commendable development from the perspective of children's rights.

The idea that education should involve a more equal relationship between parents, their children and the state is shared by few of the vocal home educating organizations. Their rejection of Badman's (2009) report, alongside the political pressures of a looming election, reduced the number of official recommendations for change. These recommendations were intended to be part of the outgoing Labour Government's Children, Schools and Families Bill (2009–10) [8], but not a single recommendation was passed in the Commons. Badman's review, then, produced no change to EHE, an outcome that disappointed many professionals and practitioners. Concerns about the effectiveness of the existing EHE system, as expressed by LAs and children's organizations, thus remain unaddressed for the time being.

Analysing the reception of Badman's review of EHE reveals how public-sector professionals perceived problems regarding EHE. Suggestions for change were strongly opposed by vocal home education organizations. The episode unearthed deep philosophical questions about who decides the nature and content of a 'suitable' education for home-educated children, and about the meaning and purpose of education in modern society (Monk, 2009). EHE is a form of education and, like school provision, it is a contested field. Still, the resulting lack of change to EHE policy and guidance means that the vague regulations regarding EHE still separate it from wider educational policies and practices. Questions about the relative rights and responsibilities of the state, parents and child, and about the systems for ensuring a suitable education for all children, remain.

Contemplating the political situation reveals that only certain voices have been heard: specifically, the powerful voices of children's service professionals and home education groups. Travellers make up a significant number of the families who continue to choose EHE as an educational pathway for their children, but there appeared to be no reference to Gypsies' or Travellers' use of EHE in Badman's review of EHE in England. There was during the review a heavy focus upon rights and child protection, but educational equality issues did not really feature. This book, then, takes up important and overlooked questions concerning EHE's relationships to educational equality and wider social justice.

The guidance, views and issues documented in this chapter are useful reminders that school is a relatively new phenomenon and that individuals have widely differing feelings about mass education. The complexity of EHE rests upon deep-rooted philosophical commitments about the nature and purpose of education. There is a continuing debate about equality, about who should be in the principal position of control in the educational lives of children and about what impact the answers may have on society (Ray, 2000). Consequently, is not advisable to examine EHE in isolation from broader educational and social issues. While differing in their perspectives, most researchers agree that the home education movement offers a fascinating critique of contemporary education systems (Gewirtz and Cribb, 2009). The point of this book is not to advocate for or against EHE or school, but to draw attention to the situations in which parents are compelled to home educate.

The main concern is that for Gypsies and Travellers the decision to home educate may be the product of racial injustice in education. Tate suggested in 1997 that race remained a significant factor in society and education in particular, a view that Gillborn (2008) and others uphold today. Research and guidance concerning EHE show that the reasons parents elect for home education are often associated with difficulties within conventional schooling (Arora, 2006; DCSF, 2007; Winstanley, 2009; Webb, 2010). Although it is acknowledged that EHE appears to offer an educational escape route from challenging school systems, it is important to consider emerging equality issues concerning Traveller families' use of EHE that reflect injustice. One emerging issue concerns Gypsies' and Traveller's experiences in school: this topic forms the focus of the next chapter.

Chapter 4

Gypsy and Traveller children in mainstream school

> My brother went to school, he left primary and went to secondary.
> At the parents evening there was no work. Mum asked why not.
> The teacher said: 'To be honest, he is so quiet we forget he is
> there'. His name was three letters long and he could not spell
> it. He was 12. So none of us went to secondary school. He got
> pulled out and we never went to big school, only the little school.
> He learnt himself to read when he was 14. He done more in two
> years than they did.
>
> (Anona)

Anona's story reminds us that we cannot consider home education without thinking about what goes on in school. To fully understand the reasons Gypsy and other Traveller families take up EHE, we need to be aware of the historic and continuing difficulties all Traveller children experience in mainstream schools. The literature on Travellers' experiences in schools unveils a deeply complex and challenging educational picture. The concern is that mainstream educational structures and attitudes play a significant part in Gypsies' and other Travellers' increasing uptake of EHE.

The historical role of Traveller Education Services

For many years now, Gypsy and Traveller children's educational underachievement has been a major concern. Almost 50 years ago the Plowden report (Department of Education and Science [DES], 1967) stated that Gypsy and other Traveller children's needs went largely unmet. The report described Traveller children as the most educationally deprived children in the country. Some 20 years later Swann (DES, 1985) reported that the educational situation in which Gypsy and Traveller children found themselves 'illustrates to an extreme degree the experience of prejudice and alienation which faces many other ethnic minority children' (DES, 1985: 740). Both reports pressed for specialist support and services: Traveller Education Services (TES) were set up in response. The earliest TESs were established in the 1970s, but only in the 1990s was centralized funding for TESs offered to LAs. A proper network of TESs then developed across the UK. Their aim was to improve the access for and integration of Gypsy and other Traveller children into mainstream education (Derrington and Kendall, 2004).

TESs support those working in schools. They offer equality training and have used innovative distance-learning strategies to support Gypsies' and Travellers' education. An example was the Electronic And Mobility Project (ELAMP), which supported online distance learning to improve educational continuity for Showmen and other highly-mobile Traveller families (D'Arcy, 2010). TESs are recognized as targeted services that have enhanced Traveller children's education experiences (Bhopal, 2001; Bhopal and Myers, 2008; United Kingdom, 2011). The Liberal Democrat peer Lord Avebury (United Kingdom, 2011) has noted that the TES is a model of good practice and was recommended as part of the EU Roma Integration Strategy.

Access and inclusion for Gypsy and Traveller children at primary level have improved markedly over the years, but the issues at secondary level have always been more complex. Retaining Gypsy and Traveller children into the secondary-age cohort and reducing the gap in their educational achievement compared with other students remains difficult. In Chapter 1, I noted concerns that, in 2003, as many as 12,000 Gypsy and Traveller children of secondary school age were missing from school and not registered in any form of education (Ofsted, 2003). Since this time the number may have grown.

The strength of the TES has been its power within LAs to advocate for Gypsy and other Travellers' educational needs. TESs today still support Traveller families and schools, working to improve Traveller children's inclusion, access and achievement within education. Unfortunately, specialized Traveller education support has declined rapidly under recent government cuts (Doherty, 2011), and many LAs sadly no longer have TES services. The axing of specialized support reflects an educational agenda in which race inequality has almost disappeared from view (Gillborn *et al.*, 2012).

Mainstream school: A space of inequality

The difficulties Gypsy and Traveller pupils have historically experienced in school are becoming better documented in accounts that focus mainly on the Gypsy, Roma and Irish Traveller communities, groups for whom data has been recorded in the Pupil Level Annual Schools Census (PLASC) since 2004. Because such pupils can now be identified in school census data, a more informed picture of their educational situation has built up. Showmen, conversely, are not recognized as ethnic minority groups; there is little data on Showmen children's attainment in school, but research has indicated that their achievement and attainment is below average (Marks, 2010).

Attainment

Within current educational policy, research and practice, measurable attainment has become an absolute priority. Testing and reporting pupil achievement is considered to be the best way to judge the effectiveness of schools, teachers and pupils (Barber and Mourshed, 2007). Yet Stobart warns that 'when a measure becomes a target, it ceases to be a good measure' (Stobart, 2008: 125). In other words, testing may be a useful part of a child's education, but it becomes unhelpful when it is made the only goal.

British education systems remain heavily focused upon performance and enhancing pupil attainment, to the extent that issues of inclusion are ignored. Attention is given to individual pupils' needs but not to social inclusion (Jordan, 2001a; Law, 2011). Where systems of testing focus attention on those children who can achieve high scores, research has shown that ethnic minority children lose out. Teachers disregard their needs. They are offered fewer opportunities to improve their attainment (Gillborn and Youdell, 2000):

> My oldest boy could not read or write when he got to secondary school. I went to talk to his teacher. I asked him if they could focus extra on his reading and writing. He said the National Curriculum would not allow it.
>
> (Marie)

Educational systems focused upon performance continue to fail a significant number of pupils, and it is unsurprising that Gypsies and Travellers – still the minority group who are most often 'out of sight and mind' (DfES, 2003: 21) – are most deprived and most at risk (DCSF, 2009b). Now, as in the past, Gypsy and Traveller children experience unequal educational opportunities. While attainment levels for most groups have improved, for Gypsy and other Traveller pupils they have deteriorated (DCSF, 2009b; the Equality and Human Rights Commission [EHRC], 2010).

Gypsy Roma and Traveller boys have the highest school exclusion rate (Foster and Norton, 2012) of all groups. Within mainstream schools, Traveller children are more likely to be identified as having a special educational need (SEN) (DfES, 2005; Wilkin *et al.*, 2010). Traveller pupils also have the lowest school attendance rate of any ethnic minority group (DfES,

2005; EHRC, 2010). There is generally a lack of understanding and respect towards Traveller children. Expectations of them are low and the rate of dropout during the secondary school phase is high (Derrington and Kendall, 2004; Wilkin *et al.*, 2009). Numerous reports and research studies have highlighted the difficulties Traveller children face in school that stop them attending and achieving. They encounter racism, bullying, discrimination, negative teacher attitudes and inconsistent or inadequate support (Lloyd and Stead, 2001; Tyler, 2005; Lloyd and McClusky, 2008; Wilkin *et al.*, 2010; Foster and Norton, 2012). It is worrying that, within educational debates, ability is frequently discussed in isolation from wider questions about social disadvantage, race inequality and educational opportunities (Gillborn, 2002), meaning that issues of racism and discrimination are seldom raised.

Racism and discrimination

Discrimination and race inequality are the main obstacles to Gypsies' and Travellers' educational success. Over the past 20 years educational reports (DES, 1985; Ofsted, 1999) and research (Lloyd *et al.*, 1999; Jordan, 2001a; Derrington and Kendall, 2004) have highlighted the nature and persistence of racism and racist name-calling experienced by Traveller children in English schools.

> They do say now 'we don't tolerate bullying' but I have experienced it and my children have. I know for a fact my children have been bullied in that school for being a Traveller. The schools won't acknowledge it but it is true. If you go to school and ask them about it they would say they do not know what I was talking about. But I am not the only Traveller in the school who has complained.
>
> (Tina)

Disappointingly, few schools have adequate knowledge about the history, culture and modern-day lifestyles of Gypsies and other Travellers. They are still too often the invisible and unfavoured minority (Jordan, 2001a). Reports of racist name-calling and physical bullying of Traveller children dominate research that seeks Travellers' views and experiences of schooling (Lloyd and McClusky, 2008). According to Traveller professionals, prejudice towards Gypsies and Travellers is everywhere (Ureche and Franks, 2007).

Showman pupils also suffer discrimination. They are usually on the road for most of the academic year and are marginalized because of their nomadic lifestyle and their association with 'Gypsies and vagabonds'

(Danaher, 2001: 3). Research (McKinney, 2001; Reynolds *et al.*, 2003; Lloyd and McClusky, 2008) shows that mainstream organizations cite the cultural characteristics of Gypsies, Travellers and Showmen as barriers to achievement. Cultural differences are thus used to blame Gypsies and Travellers for their difficulties in accessing public services: when this blaming happens in the context of education, it provides mainstream education systems with an excuse for doing nothing about the racism and discrimination that prevails. The uptake of EHE among Gypsy and other Traveller communities illustrates a consequence of this misplaced blame, as such communities opt out of educational systems that blame them for their own exclusion.

Low expectations and secondary school dropout

Expectations of Gypsy and other Traveller children's educational aspirations and achievement in school are generally low, especially around the time of transition to secondary school (Derrington and Kendall, 2004, 2008; Derrington, 2007). This transition is certainly an issue for highly mobile Travellers (Marks and Rowlands, 2010). Showman families travel throughout the year: on the road from February to November or even December, their children do not necessarily start at their new secondary schools when the academic year begins in September. By the time families return from travelling and their children begin secondary school, friendship groups among other pupils have already been established. The Showman children alone are the new ones. The later highly mobile students start secondary school, the harder it is for them to fit in. Improving educational outcomes consequently becomes particularly serious for secondary-aged Showman pupils.

Transition to secondary school is a key point when many Traveller children besides Showmen also drop out of the education system. Even when Gypsy and other Traveller children do transfer from primary to secondary school, retention can be problematic. Recent research has shown that, nationally, only one in five Gypsy and Traveller children completes secondary school (Wilkin *et al.*, 2010). In 2007 Ureche and Franks undertook a research study into the views and identities of 201 Roma, Gypsy and Traveller young people and found that the average age of school dropout was 11.49 years. Over a third had 'dropped out from school by the time they reached 10 and three quarters by the time they were 13' (Ureche and Franks, 2007: 32). A similar picture was evident in the sample of Romany Gypsy and Showman families I interviewed. Among the 11 families interviewed there were 15 children in total who were currently being home educated; six of these had left school at the secondary transition stage or early on in secondary school. Two left in Year 10 with only one full year to complete secondary school. Three left in primary school.

The dropout situation in some European countries is even more worrying. The reasons for dropout vary from country to country. In Slovenia over 70 per cent of Roma pupils never finish primary school and only 3 per cent finish secondary school (Baclija, 2008). In Bulgaria, schools refer cases of school dropout to social workers but have no capacity to deal proactively with such cases. Many countries lack monitoring systems to check attendance, meaning the scale of the problem is not recognized and goes unaddressed. Complex reasons underpin school dropout. They include issues of race and racism, family poverty, rural living locations and access to quality education establishments. Research suggests that being Roma significantly increases the probability of dropout (Bruggemann, 2012).

Failure to include Gypsies, Roma and Travellers in mainstream schooling in the UK and Europe severely obstructs their educational needs and restricts their long-term prospects. The use of scripts, as recent research shows, is one of the biggest challenges regarding secondary transition. Wilkin *et al.* define a script as 'a common response or phrase which may be consciously or unconsciously applied as a form of personal or cultural observation, defence or protection' (Wilkin *et al.*, 2010: 108). In my research I have heard these scripts in use: some Traveller families state that secondary school attendance is not commonplace within Traveller culture. Beyond this, I argue that such scripts are also employed by schools. Below is a young Show-woman's story that illustrates the effect of scripts:

> I was gifted and talented at primary school. I loved the little school. I was top in every class there. If we was travelling they would send me work-packs. I did them because I wanted to. I liked learning. The school was not racist. At secondary though … you were just a number, not a pupil. I wanted to go till the end. I did textiles; it was another choice if I did not want to choose the Showmen lifestyle. The textile teacher would not give me work though. She told me just to work on the computer. I did that work and that surprised her. I think they had made their mind up about what I was going be … they thought I did not need school and had decided on my career already.
>
> (Caprice)

Caprice's story and the literature on Gypsy and other Travellers' experiences in school highlight many problems with an educational system where stereotypes and misunderstandings of Traveller communities are common (Wilkin *et al.*, 2009). Lloyd and McClusky (2008) suggest that central to the negative educational experiences of so many Travellers lies a denial of difference and of the complexities of cultural identities. Accounts of Travellers' failure in education commonly emphasize Travellers' reluctance to participate in education, and this is presented as a feature of Traveller cultures (Piper and Garratt, 2005; Wilkin *et al.*, 2010). Yosso (2006) describes this position as 'deficit thinking', whereby minority students are seen to be at fault for their poor performance. This, Yosso warns, is one of the most prevalent forms of contemporary racism. Showmen's marginalization often arises from their being viewed as different and deviant: 'sometimes they don't understand that we're more or less like them but just travel on' (Showman child in Danaher, 1995: 43). Wyer *et al.* (1997) warn that it is important not to underestimate the detrimental effect of teachers' blinkered perceptions of some pupils and the way these perceptions obstruct children's education.

Gypsy and other Traveller children can face difficulties in negotiating the disconnections between home and school cultures (Wilkin *et al.*, 2010), experiencing what Derrington and Kendall call 'cultural dissonance'. These authors describe cultural dissonance as 'a sense of discord or disharmony experienced by individuals, where cultural differences are unexpected, unexplained and therefore difficult to negotiate' (Derrington and Kendall, 2008: 125). Kiddle (1999) describes Showman children's cultural experiences of home and school as an effort to exist between two worlds; the education system is focused on a very narrow set of indicators that define success and failure, meaning that schools seldom appreciate the breadth of cultural knowledge and skills that many Traveller children have. Moreover, as Levinson and Sparkes suggest, the 'different demands of home and school can lead to feelings of cultural dislocation and anxiety' (Levinson and Sparkes, 2006: 79).

Wyer *et al.* (1997) suggest that the experience of cultural dissonance requires children to negotiate 'border crossings' between cultures. Accordingly, many Traveller students resort to specific coping strategies in school, trying to deal with both cultural dissonance and their social exclusion. Derrington (2007) suggests that these strategies, often maladaptive, can be summarized as 'fight, flight and playing White'. Fight strategies, consisting of physical and verbal retaliation to racial abuse, often result in Traveller students' exclusion from school (Lloyd *et al.*, 1999; Ofsted, 1999; Derrington, 2007). Time after time I witnessed Gypsy or Traveller children being excluded for fighting, while the children who called them 'dirty Gyppos' remained in school.

Flight strategies include Gypsies' and other Travellers' low attendance and self-imposed exclusion: if you do not feel that you belong in a system, you may want to withdraw. Traveller children have the highest levels of non-attendance at school of all groups (Foster and Norton, 2012). I would count EHE within the 'flight' category, as it is a method of escaping the school system and the difficulties created there. Strategies that constitute 'playing White' involve concealing one's ethnicity or denying one's heritage – hiding who you really are. Gypsies and other Travellers fairly commonly avoid telling others about their ethnicity or culture as a way of coping with deep-rooted racism in schools and other institutions (Derrington, 2007).

Considering all the difficulties Traveller children have to contend with in school makes clear how attractive EHE might be in representing a much safer educational space. Kiddle's 'two worlds' analogy is highly applicable to EHE for Gypsies and other Travellers: it illuminates the gap between home and school, with EHE located as a potentially more positive educational space within this gap.

Traveller children's experience in education reflects the discrimination they face in the wider society. School represents a microcosm of society for young Travellers: it is a place where racism, prejudice and cultural invisibility are commonplace. Indeed, Drudy and Lynch (1993) suggest that, for Travellers, the problem is that schools expect Traveller children to adapt to their static timetable and curricula, even though these systems inherently exclude Traveller cultures and lifestyles. The deficit thinking about Travellers within the literature has been noted, and reflects the way schools code Traveller children's difficulties as products of cultural difference (Yosso, 2006). Negative cultural generalizations indicate how Traveller communities in England are continually castigated and thought to be undeserving. Jordan (2001a) observes that the attitude that Gypsies and other Travellers 'bring it on themselves' means that little educational response is directed towards their needs.

Although research on Showmen's children is sparse, Danaher's (1995, 2001) research from Australia is revealing. Danaher suggests that, for these children, schools can be uncomfortable places, 'at best temporary resting stops on the show circuit, at worst dehumanised environments' (Danaher, 1995: 13). Kiddle reported on Showmen families' accounts of school in England, where parents complained that children were sat at the back of class, given some colouring to do and ignored, or brought to the front to tell the class about life on the fairground. For the majority school was 'a sad waste of time and opportunity' (Kiddle, 1999: 99). The picture of education for Travellers is complex and Showmen, like minority ethnic groups, are marginalized on account of deficit cultural assumptions.

The prevailing, oversimplified rhetoric concerning cultural difference masks inequalities and allows education systems to abdicate responsibility for meeting Traveller needs. Wilkin *et al.* (2010) suggest that many schools still attribute the low attainment figures for Traveller pupils to parental and community attitudes. The same issues are reported in eastern European contexts.

The educational situation for Roma in Europe

The barriers to Roma children's access and inclusion in education in continental Europe are similar to those in the UK, although more extreme. Poverty, exclusion, segregation, assimilation to the majority culture or dismissal of their culture and identity, prejudice and discrimination remain the most significant issues (Macura-Milovanovic and Pecek, 2013). Roma, Gypsy and Traveller communities form the largest ethnic minority within the enlarged European Union. Roma are also the fastest-growing minority in central and eastern Europe; they tend to be concentrated in the poorest countries (Save the Children, 2001). The European Commission (2011) has estimated that there are around 12 million Roma in Europe.

Roma are said to be ten times poorer than the majority population in Europe. Poor living conditions, lack of regular income, unemployment among adults, lack of social assistance, low literacy levels and high numbers of children in families are among the difficulties that continue to marginalize Roma. Roma remain socially excluded and are discriminated against in all countries, albeit to differing degrees. Educational achievement among Roma in Europe, as in the UK, is low, and this is due largely to the segregation of Roma communities from the majority population (European Commission, 2004; Ivanov *et al.*, 2006).

Most Roma in central European countries complete primary education (from 6 to 12 years of age), but a large number in southeast Europe do not. In Montenegro, Albania and Moldova, over 30 per cent of young Roma (aged 14–20) have not completed primary education (Bruggemann, 2012). Many Roma across eastern Europe are educationally segregated, often streamed into special schools or classes and thus overrepresented in such provision. Another type of segregation occurs where Roma pupils make up the majority of the school community in a regular school; these then become 'ghetto schools' as non-Roma parents tend to withdraw their children. Sixty per cent of Roma pupils in the Czech Republic and 30 per cent in Hungary attend ethnically segregated schools. Standards of teaching and facilities in both these kinds of segregated schooling are often poor (Wilkin *et al.*, 2009).

One reason for Roma children's segregation into special education schools is that they may not speak the official language of instruction on arrival at a school. They are thus segregated due to language barriers, not any cognitive impairments. Research (Miskovic, 2013) has shown, however, that even after Roma pupils learn the local language they are seldom returned to mainstream education. One reason Roma children may not have acquired the official language of school instruction is that very few access early years education or kindergarten. Early care and childhood education positively influence educational attainment and outcomes at later stages (Bruggemann, 2012), yet in Bulgaria and Serbia, for example, priority in pre-school access is granted to children of employed parents (Bruggemann, 2012; Murushiakova *et al.*, 2007). Child protection departments and schools seem to be reluctant or helpless to involve Romani children in pre-school or kindergarten (Kukova, 2011). Other obstacles include the cost of attendance or the distance rural families need to travel to get to school. When Roma families do try to enrol for pre-school, their children are often segregated into a special education setting with poorer teaching and fewer resources. There is also evidence of overt discrimination, where heads of pre-school settings simply do not allow Roma to enrol their children (Open Society Institute, 2007).

Recent research highlights the ways in which teachers continue to ignore and thus sustain prejudice and discrimination against Roma children. Roma families have explained their reluctance to let their children go to school: they fear abuse by non-Roma children and abduction for marriage, or may lack the clothes, shoes and transportation the children need to get to school (Kukova, 2011). But research indicates that the majority of student teachers in Serbia and Slovenia attribute Roma children's underachievement to their lack of motivation, their parents' lack of interest in school and the fact that Roma pupils are not accepted by their peers (Macura-Milovanovic and Pecek, 2013).

Though the aspirations of Roma are high compared to the real outcomes, there is a general assumption – as Bruggemann (2012) explains – that the Roma's educational marginalization results from a lack of aspirations. In eastern Europe, cultural differences are also used to explain the purported low educational aspirations of the Roma. Although an aspiration gap does exist between Roma and non-Roma, Bruggemann suggests the reasons for this are more likely to lie in Roma individuals' greater poverty and hopelessness; Roma expect to be discriminated against in the workplace, so assume they will gain less from education (O'Higgins, 2010). Bruggemann (2012) warns therefore that, though, traditional cultural values may play a role in reducing aspirations, any assumptions regarding correlation between cultural difference and school disaffection should be treated with caution.

The picture of Traveller education in the UK is certainly better than in some eastern European countries, especially in matters of intercultural practice – educational practice involving, or representing, different cultures (Wilkin *et al.*, 2009). Yet the discrimination and racism that Gypsies, Travellers and Roma experience is very similar to that documented in continental Europe, albeit less extreme. Many teachers are confused about what Gypsy, Roma and other Traveller cultures actually embody. They may therefore either deny that difference exists or construct it as something deviant (Lloyd and Norris, 1998). Achieving inclusive education in schools is challenging and the process to secure it is often misunderstood. For example, when Rousseau and Tate asked teachers about their response to the needs of increasingly diverse student populations, teachers universally described 'treating students equally, as [being] their approach for ensuring equity' (Rousseau and Tate, 2003: 14), ignoring the importance of equality of outcome.

Ultimately, it is the approaches that individual schools adopt that determine whether Traveller children fail or succeed in mainstream systems (Derrington and Kendall, 2004). In their longitudinal research following Traveller children from primary through to secondary school, Derrington and Kendall used the terms 'Oaks' and 'Willows' to describe contrasting school approaches. The Oaks demonstrated unbending and inflexible approaches towards individual Traveller children's needs, whereas the Willows were more flexible and receptive to the needs of all children. Research reports suggest that Traveller children make progress equal to their peers when conditions are right. Traveller children want to learn, but the barriers in the educational system often prevent them from succeeding (Warrington, 2006; D'Arcy, 2008, 2010; DCSF, 2009b).

Under the recent Labour Government a number of publications and research reports were commissioned to promote examples of good practice in schools. In House of Lords discussion of the new Education Bill 2011, Lord Avebury commented that 'good intentions have done little for Traveller children over the past 50 years and governments have yet to match their deeds to their words' (United Kingdom, House of Lords, June 14, 2011:

Column 709). Focusing on the needs of marginalized communities is clearly not the same as responding to those needs (Craig *et al.*, 2012).

Summing up this chapter, there is a significant body of literature that concentrates on the poor educational experiences and outcomes experienced by Gypsy and other Traveller children in school. Interestingly, within educational policy, the predominant issue concerning Traveller children's education is often low attainment in school, prompting efforts to drive up teaching standards for these groups. Yet research substantiates the idea that the most important actions are those that encourage Traveller children to attend in the first place, and that these include preventing discrimination and securing Traveller children's social and emotional well-being. Wilkin *et al.* (2010) suggest that schools need to understand fully that Traveller pupils are unlikely to achieve or even attend if they are unhappy in school. Lloyd and McClusky suggest that concerns about the preservation of cultural and family values, and well-founded fears of bullying and assault in school, mean that many Travellers in Britain 'wish, but do still not feel able, to participate fully in state education, particularly at secondary school level' (Lloyd and McClusky, 2008: 336). Thus, Gypsies' and Travellers' experiences in school make EHE an attractive educational alternative. The next chapter offers a critical overview of the position of home education as an alternative educational space to school.

Chapter 5
Gypsies, Travellers and EHE
The tales told

> The mental age of an average adult Gypsy is thought to be about that of a child of ten. Gypsies have never accomplished anything of great significance in writing, painting, musical composition, science or social organization. Quarrelsome, quick to anger or laughter, they are unthinkingly but not deliberately cruel. Loving bright colours, they are ostentatious and boastful, but lack bravery.
>
> (*Encyclopedia Britannica*, 1954, cited in Bowers, 2012)

This startling description of the Gypsy community was published in the *Encyclopedia Britannica* in 1954. To suggest that Gypsies and other Travellers have accomplished nothing of great significance in the arts and sciences is simply incorrect. Many Gypsies and Travellers have contributed a great deal, but their ethnicity and cultural background is not always revealed at the time of their successes. Sir Charlie Chaplin, Sir Michael Caine and Bob Hoskins, Nobel Prize winner Mother Theresa, and footballers Eric Cantona and Freddy Eastwood are all Gypsies. The singers David Essex, Cher, Elvis Presley and Adam Ant are also said to have had Romanichel origins (Leicestershire Together, 2013). Gypsy and Traveller people are as brave as any; thousands of Gypsy and Traveller men died fighting for Britain in the Second World War, while Roma from all over Europe were detained in prison camps. It is not known exactly how many European Roma were killed in the Holocaust, but historians have estimated that the total amounted to a quarter of the entire community (Kenrick and Puxon, 1995).

I still show professionals and students the quote above and ask them to guess when it was written. Feedback suggests that people would not be surprised if it was published as recently as 10 years ago. We are familiar with and even tolerant of derogatory language about Gypsies and other Travellers, when if it was used in relation to most other groups or communities there would be outrage. Trevor Phillips, when Chair of the Commission for Racial Equality (CRE), famously described racism towards Travellers as 'the last respectable form of racism' (BBC, 2004).

We learn to believe that a person's race can offer clues about that individual and his or her behaviour, unaware that ideologies and stereotypes often shape our initial impressions and judgements. Those very beliefs are embedded in our education systems.

(Zamudio *et al.*, 2011: 3)

Racist beliefs and deficit thinking about Gypsies and Travellers are embedded in our education systems, practices and in the literature. This chapter provides examples from the literature on EHE to illuminate the more subtle and hidden forms of racism that sustain discrimination against Gypsies and other Travellers.

Racism and discrimination

Racism is complex and ever-changing. The *Oxford English Dictionary* defines racism as 'the belief that all members of each race possess characteristics, abilities, or qualities specific to that race, especially so as to distinguish it as inferior or superior to another race or races' ('Racism', 2012). Because racist speech and actions are no longer legal, some might assume that racism itself no longer exists. We may overlook obvious forms of racism. Slavery has indeed been abolished in developed countries and segregation on the basis of skin colour is against the law, but this does not mean racism has disappeared. New racisms have emerged. Chattoo and Atkin (2012) argue that racism, as originally defined by its focus on racial characteristics, has been replaced by cultural racism. Cultural racism sees cultural and religious difference as a threat to national identity and dominant white cultural values.

One example of cultural racism is Islamophobia, the hatred of Muslim people and their religion (Housee, 2012: 106). Islam is seen as separate and Other; it is treated as though it lacks values in common with other cultures, is not affected by them and does not influence them (Runnymede Trust, 1997). Islamophobia is a form of racism that excludes and marginalizes populations not on the basis of their biological differences but on their so-called incommensurable cultural differences (Housee, 2012: 106). This new type of racism concerns itself with culture and identity.

Cultural racism is not a new phenomenon, but it is a matter for concern as it focuses upon cultural difference. This means that those who espouse culturally racist views claim that they are not racist on grounds that race plays no obvious part in the language used. Barker (1981: 18) explains that individuals expressing culturally racist views may not think of themselves as superior: 'You do not even need to dislike or blame those who are so different from you ... in order to say that the presence of these aliens constitutes a threat to our way of life'. Cultural racism, then, is not necessarily conscious, as the language is different from that usually associated with discrimination on the grounds of racial characteristics. The mindset of inferiority and superiority, though, remains the same.

Asylum seekers, Roma communities, eastern Europeans and refugees are all labelled in culturally racist discourse as Others who do not belong. Their presence or arrival is depicted in the media as a threat to British life and acted upon in social policies. Cultural racism is found also in education. The notion of Gypsies' and Travellers' cultural differences is perpetuated through the mainstream literature about EHE in England. Here, I analyse the references to Gypsies and Travellers in a recent Ofsted report (2010) regarding LAs and home education, in a summary of evidence related to EHE in the UK (DCSF, 2009a) and finally in a book on elective home education in the UK (Webb, 2010). I ask critical questions and challenge some of the statements made, highlighting how Gypsies' and Travellers' cultural differences are used as an excuse to avoid responsibility for their educational needs.

EHE and Travellers: The dominant discourses
Local Authorities and Home Education *(Ofsted, 2010)*

The Ofsted report (2010) aimed to evaluate how well 15 LAs discharged their duties towards home-educated children and young people. Ofsted officials consulted members of public body departments, including LA staff and headteachers. Ofsted held meetings for home-educating parents and their children and received questionnaire responses from parents and children.

The first criticism of this study is rather general. The processes and people that Ofsted involved in their study are revealing: Ofsted concentrated upon talking with professionals from mainstream education, rather than experts on home education. In this book's opening chapter, I suggested that judgements of EHE provision are often based on mainstream school standards. There is a trend towards consultation with school professionals rather than EHE experts, and this tendency is evidenced in this report.

It is also not clear from the report which parents Ofsted talked to about EHE, although the report states that group meetings were arranged to confer with home-educating parents. Experience suggests that such meetings rarely include so-called hard-to-reach groups, such as Gypsies and Travellers. Traveller communities may not read public notices or receive questionnaires, as they often live in geographically isolated areas. Moreover, the levels of literacy within the adult Gypsy and Traveller community (EHRC, 2010) limit the capacity of members of these communities to make the written responses they might wish to. Consultation with Traveller communities requires outreach because an open door strategy, whereby all are welcome, is not in itself enough to ensure that they access provision. The service provided is in effect closed to anyone who does not know about it and has no prior relationship with it (Save the Children, 2007). Outreach activities, whereby services actively canvas the input of their community and professionals visit families face to face, are time-consuming and more expensive than sending out questionnaires or displaying public notices inviting people to a meeting. The point is that the way people are invited to be consulted affects the makeup of the home-educating parents and children represented. Open group meetings are unlikely to encapsulate all those engaged with EHE within an LA under study.

Secondly, the report's single reference to Gypsy, Roma and Traveller families is inaccurate. The quote below alludes to an urban LA where 15 out of 31 home-educating families were Gypsies, Roma or Travellers:

> Some Traveller, Gypsy and Roma families chose home education so that they could continue children's education whilst travelling. The Travellers' Education Service in all the authorities visited were well aware of the specific needs of these groups and were striving to support them flexibly and effectively.
>
> (Ofsted, 2010: 7)

This claim is controversial for two reasons: its over-simplification of the issues of travelling, and its over-emphasis on the role of TESs. First, although mobility issues still affect access and attendance for some Traveller children (particularly highly mobile families, such as Showmen), many families today lead less nomadic lifestyles (Ivatts, 2006). This is not to suggest that mobility is not an issue for learning continuity, but the assumption here is that *all* Travellers are mobile. This presumption obscures issues of racism and discrimination and blames Traveller children's low attendance and achievement in school on the communities themselves (Wilkin *et al.*, 2010). Research indicates that mobility is no longer the most important factor regarding Travellers' education (Derrington and Kendall, 2004; Wilkin *et al.*, 2010).

Of course, some families may indeed use EHE to continue learning while travelling; travel is indeed part of the history of Gypsies and Travellers, whose ancestors journeyed from India to Europe, the UK and beyond, so there is certainly some truth to the common stereotype of the travelling Gypsy (Hancock, 2002). Many Roma, Gypsies, Travellers and Showmen still travel today for work purposes. But others may travel not because they choose to but because they are forced to do so, by laws that forbid them to stop in public places and by a drastic shortage of site provision. It is important, therefore, to remember that some families travel because they have little choice but to keep moving on.

This Ofsted report makes no reference to the reasons why those who are home educating travel. Neither is there mention of why other Traveller families, those not travelling, chose EHE. Fifty per cent of the total EHE population were Travellers, so one might have expected the authors to include these families in their consultation, yet there is no indication that they did so.

Secondly, there is an assumption that TESs deal with all Traveller issues, whereas in fact EHE is not usually within most Traveller Education Services' remit. TESs are funded to improve attendance, achievement and attainment within mainstream schooling (Bhopal and Myers, 2008).

Reflecting the rhetoric of cultural difference, the Ofsted report suggests that mobility is a key reason for EHE among Travellers. But the failure to gather any evidence from the Traveller community itself, and the subsequent reliance on stereotypical propaganda about Traveller communities and Traveller Education Services alike, signals this as an example of subtle but nonetheless clear cultural racism. Cultural stereotypes of Gypsies and other Travellers function not only as a form of victim-blaming but also embody a reframing of historical and contemporary cause-and-effect that obscures race and renders it neutral (Dixson and Rousseau, 2005; DePouw, 2012). Attention needs to be paid to the real reasons Travellers home educate, and the oppressive structures and attitudes that exist within society and school warrant critical analysis.

Still, Ofsted's overall findings about the reasons parents home educate were interesting. Most home-educated children they consulted had attended school; a third of parent respondents had removed their children from school because of bullying. One-quarter of the home-educated children were reported to have SEN and had been withdrawn, as their parents believed their needs were not being met. These reasons connect with other research on EHE (Arora, 2006; Gabb, 2004). They indicate a relationship between issues in school and the uptake of EHE.

'Elective Home Education: An overview of evidence' (DCSF, 2009a)
In 2009 the Schools Analysis and Research Division of the DCSF compiled a summary of evidence on the subject of EHE in the UK. The report makes occasional reference to Gypsies and other Travellers. It discusses the high proportion of Gypsies and Travellers engaging with EHE and the increasing number of them opting for EHE. It highlights the fact that twice as many

secondary-aged Gypsy and Traveller children are home educated as those of primary age. The report also notes specific reasons for uptake of EHE among Traveller communities. These include 'a fear of cultural erosion, a judged lack of relevance with the secondary school curriculum and the fear of racist and other bullying' (DCSF, 2009a: 3). This information comes from a report by Ivatts (discussed below), but it is not referenced. The DCSF report then quotes a section of Ivatts' (2006) research:

> An investigation of Traveller home educated children found that few parents of these children have knowledge, skills and resources to provide or deliver full time education that is efficient and suitable.
>
> (Ivatts, 2006, cited in DCSF, 2009a: 8)

This selective citation is misleading, as Ivatts's point is clarified in the paragraph that follows in his original report:

> … And yet the percentage of Gypsy/Roma and Traveller families who have opted for EHE is increasing at a high rate. There may also be a possible 50% to 75% of children from these communities opting out of secondary education. Given the research findings about school curricular irrelevance and racist bullying, the developing situation re EHE is a clear example of racial discrimination and social exclusion.
>
> (Ivatts, 2006: 22)

Debates regarding race and racism are often hidden from view (Craig *et al.*, 2012). Not publishing all the evidence of the racism directed at Gypsies and other Travellers means that the issues are diluted and ignored. Such selective representation also portrays Traveller communities as deviant and lacking care and interest in their child's education.

In his own report, Ivatts (2006) warns readers to be aware of interpretations of his study. He highlights his concern with the 'creation and or confirmation of stereotypes either positive or negative' within short research reports that are constrained by word count limits (Ivatts, 2006: 106). He makes clear that his report should not be interpreted as a criticism of Traveller families or the provision of EHE, yet the DCSF uses his work to do precisely this.

Elective Home Education in the UK *(Webb, 2010)*

Webb's (2010) book, *Elective Home Education in the UK*, contains very few references to Gypsies or Travellers. Nonetheless, within the half-page or so that covers Gypsy and Traveller home educators, Webb makes many unfounded claims. First, he suggests that it is a concern that many Traveller children are home educated. He does not state why or who holds this concern.

Secondly, he states that 'traditionally, this group [Travellers] value practical skills over academic achievement' (Webb, 2010: 103). Webb's statement is not referenced or justified. It reflects a derogatory picture of Traveller communities as one homogeneous group. It reminds me of the *Encyclopedia Britannica* quote with which this chapter opened. Given the significant body of research literature confirming that Travellers do want their children to be educated (Acton, 2004; Lloyd and McClusky, 2008; Wilkin *et al.*, 2010) and the lack of information on the actual numbers and practices of home-educated Traveller children, it seems dangerous for him to have reached such a firm conclusion about the reasons why Gypsies and Travellers home educate.

Thirdly, Webb suggests that the monitoring of Travellers' home education provision is hampered by their semi-nomadic lifestyle. Webb also refers to Travellers' high rates of absence and exclusions. Again, no explanation is given for these two statements, nor for why he places them together in the text. In my view, they confirm his over-reliance on cultural assumptions rather than informed research. Research with highly mobile Traveller families highlights that mobility is an issue in learning progression but that parents still advocate education (D'Arcy, 2008). Ivatts (2006) confirmed that mobility was not a significant causal factor for uptake of EHE, as has the work of Derrington and Kendall (2004) and Wilkin *et al.* (2010). This establishes that mobility is no longer the main reason for Travellers' low rates of attendance and high rates of exclusion. Actually it is discrimination against Travellers and the feeling of being alienated from the system that lies behind this community's uptake of EHE. As Derrington and Kendall suggest, 'individuals who feel isolated, socially and culturally are unlikely to reach their full potential' (Derrington and Kendall, 2004: 178).

Webb (2010) also categorizes Travellers, along with Muslims, Christians and Jews, as people who may choose to home educate for religious or cultural reasons. There may be some cultural aspects related to these communities' decisions to home educate but Webb relies for this claim on anecdotal evidence from home educating groups' Internet lists that 'suggest that a fair number of Muslims are also choosing to educate their children at home for religious and cultural reasons' (Webb, 2010: 35). This is a clear example of the way in which those who are culturally different are placed apart from the norm, implying deviance.

Webb proposes that there is a suspicion that Traveller girls are not provided with any formal education after the age of 11 and that this point was raised by the Children, Schools and Families Select Committee (2010) as part of the Badman review. It has not been possible to find such a reference. Professional experience indicates that it is certainly not the case that all Traveller girls drop out at the point of transition to secondary school. Many complete their education and one young traveller woman recently graduated from Cambridge University with a top degree (Attewill, 2013).

Thus we see that mainstream literature continues to send out negative and often inaccurate messages about Gypsies, Travellers and education. Worryingly inaccurate and inappropriate messages are then communicated to readers. This is how cultural racism persists. These texts reflect the general way in which Traveller communities are labelled as different and deviant, and the over-reliance on stereotypical assumptions about them. Thompson rightly suggests that it is unhelpful to have an 'over-reliance on cultural explanations for educational issues as this distracts attention from significant emotional factors and structural factors such as class and race' (Thompson, 1997: 71). Moreover, the focus on Traveller culture implicitly associates educational problems with the cultural practices and behaviours of the Other rather than with the failure of policy makers and education providers to understand and engage with difference (Craig *et al.*, 2012).

This critique of the literature confirms the urgent need for accurate research about EHE and Travellers' experiences of this educational alternative. Two other studies on this subject are noteworthy: one commissioned by the Department of Education and Skills (DfES) and written by an expert in the field of Traveller education (Ivatts, 2006) and one commissioned by Hampshire County Council into the use of EHE for Traveller children in their county (Bhopal and Myers, 2009a). These two reports highlight the links between racism and discrimination in school and Gypsy and Travellers' uptake of EHE. They tell an informed story about Travellers, schools and EHE. They also provide a counter-story to the mainstream literature just discussed.

The situation regarding the current policy, provision and practice in Elective Home Education for Gypsy, Roma and Traveller children (*Ivatts, 2006*)

In November 2004 the DfES initiated a small-scale research project to investigate Gypsies', Roma's and Travellers' use of EHE, in response to reports from the Traveller Education Services (TES) that EHE uptake was rising among Traveller communities. Ivatts sent out two detailed questionnaires to the people responsible for EHE within 23 LAs and their TESs. The analysis of responses indicated that 16–35 per cent of those who had opted for EHE within the sample areas were Gypsy, Roma and Traveller children, and that the rate of uptake of EHE among Traveller communities had increased year on year by approximately 40 per cent.

Nearly half of the sample LAs (and 94 per cent of their TESs) expressed concerns about the suitability of Gypsies' and other Travellers' EHE provision. The reasons they gave included Gypsy and Traveller parents' sometimes limited motivation, commitment and enthusiasm for education and their own limited academic skills and capacity to assess their children's educational needs, attitudes and aspirations. These negative observations of Travellers' use of EHE by those who seek to support the community may cause some surprise, but they reflect the concerns held about educational equality as well as the problem of judging EHE by school standards. TESs are funded to improve access to mainstream provision; their aim is to ensure that Traveller children can access and achieve in schools. EHE's position as a legal educational alternative can make it even harder to support Gypsy and Traveller children to stay in school.

EHE uptake can be triggered by tensions between the promotion of inclusion and the drive to secure academic success in mainstream education – a debate already familiar in the special needs world (Jordan, 2001b). Jordan suggests that state education can rarely meet the needs of all its learners and that, unfortunately, few service providers listen with respect and act supportively to uphold the views of parents. It is thus understandable that Traveller parents, and other parents, may lack motivation, enthusiasm and commitment towards schooling.

Ivatts's research is refreshing in that he does not focus upon cultural differences or Travellers' implied deviance. Instead Ivatts challenges the deficit portrayal of Gypsies and other Travellers and directs attention at the problems they experience in schools. He reports that the reasons Traveller families choose EHE are diverse. Many Gypsies and Travellers use EHE to avoid school, it is true, but this is not because of a lack of interest in their child's education or the fear of prosecution. The main reasons are 'a fear of cultural erosion, a judged lack of relevance within the secondary school curriculum and the fear of racist and other bullying' (Ivatts, 2006: 4).

Ivatts confirms that Gypsies' and Travellers' decisions to take up EHE may be the product of racial injustice in school, a conclusion shared by other researchers since. Ureche and Franks (2007) reported that the Traveller children they spoke to missed going to school once they were withdrawn for EHE and that some attributed their leaving full-time education directly to the bullying they experienced. The authors suggest that '[i]t is clearly unacceptable that any child should feel so vulnerable at school that their parents feel they have to withdraw them and teach them at home' (Ureche and Franks, 2007).

Derrington and Kendall (2004) have proposed that EHE:

> ... is a mechanism by which parents can avoid prosecution but still not send their children to secondary school and, conversely it is a way the LA and 'Gauje' society can deal with Traveller students' non-attendance at secondary school.[1]
>
> (Derrington and Kendall, 2004: 142)

In other words, EHE allows Gypsies and other Traveller children to drop out of mainstream school, or 'slip through the net' (ibid.: 142) with ease, which is convenient for schools and parents alike. Allowing children to leave school because it is convenient is clearly unacceptable. Ivatts argues that we need to look at the reasons why these families are choosing EHE, contending that it is a case of discrimination within mainstream education that illustrates how schools fail to meet the needs of Gypsies and other Traveller children. Ivatts's study confirmed that the 'practicalities of a nomadic lifestyle were not seen as a significant causal factor for most families' (Ivatts, 2006: 4) and offers a good counter-story to the dominant discourses, in which mobility is presented as the main reason for EHE uptake among Gypsies and Travellers and racism is ignored. His study exposed the need for a renewed focus on racism in education.

'A pilot study to investigate the use of elective home education for Gypsy, Roma and Traveller children in Hampshire' (Bhopal and Myers, 2009a)

Bhopal and Myers (2009a) were commissioned by Hampshire LA to examine the use of EHE by Travellers in that county. Six Traveller parents and four professionals were interviewed. Bhopal and Myers (2009a: 8) noted that parents gave two basic reasons for home educating:

- dissatisfaction with the type of schooling available;
- positive benefits from receiving a home education.

These reasons were not mutually exclusive. Bhopal and Myers reported that every family in their sample was fearful about their children's vulnerability in secondary school. Moreover, the cultural values of the school were very different to their own. Interestingly, these researchers also found that the professionals' views on why Traveller families took up EHE did not accord with the reasons cited by Travellers themselves. Professionals referred to the problems of bullying and name-calling in school and to a lack of understanding of Traveller cultures. But they all stressed that the highly mobile nature of Traveller families was the key factor – all of the professionals assumed that Traveller families were moving around. Yet a mobile lifestyle 'was not a reason given by any of the families interviewed, *none* of whom currently lived mobile lives' (Bhopal and Myers, 2009a: 12).

These professionals were apparently ill-informed about their local Traveller families or relying on cultural stereotypes to explain Travellers' reasons for home educating. Ivatts noted that, among his respondents, only 56 per cent of responsible officers had attended in-service training on EHE and only 36 per cent had attended any training on Gypsy/Roma and Traveller communities (Ivatts, 2006: 5). These research findings illustrate the dangers of relying on professional advocacy on behalf of the marginalized. They stress the importance of listening to Gypsies' and Travellers' own voices.

The researchers also remarked on the differences found in EHE practice between the six families. Four families used tutors to cover a wide range of curriculum topics. One family employed a tutor to teach curriculum-based subjects for an hour or two per week; the father in this family was also teaching his sons the family business, rather in the manner of an apprenticeship. The less affluent families were hampered by a lack of resources. Two mothers had only a laptop and some photocopied materials, which were inappropriate for the children's ages. These families had tried to access practical work experience or training for their children, but as one parent told Bhopal and Myers (2009b), 'I couldn't get nobody to take him on'. They were worried that their children were not receiving a suitable home education. Bhopal and Myers report families' constant desire for more resources, such as help with tutoring costs. Families viewed the lack of resources and support for EHE as a 'perpetuation of school provision that fails to address their needs' (ibid.: 4). Thus, parents felt that both school and EHE systems were failing their children. The authors therefore recommended that there be more support and resourcing for EHE, particularly for low-income families, to ensure their children received a suitable education.

Bhopal and Myers's research is valuable in documenting some Gypsy and Traveller parents' voices and views about EHE and wider educational debates. Of particular interest is that one family described secondary school life as unsafe and immoral, whereas their 'own Gypsy culture was understood in terms of a moral and safe world' (Bhopal and Myers, 2009a: 8). Bhopal and Myers's findings thus seem to corroborate Kiddle's. In sum, Travellers' decisions to take up EHE are based not on a rejection of school, but on their concerns about school. EHE represents a safe educational space for Traveller families, but their fears and concerns about their child's welfare in school raises important questions about equality in education.

Overall, the general EHE literature reflects a deficit view of Gypsies' and Travellers' use of EHE. The research by Bhopal and Myers and by Ivatts provides important counter-stories to the dominant accounts. Their work substantiates the reality that for Gypsies and other Travellers the decision to home educate is often a reaction to racial injustice in school. The reasons these families take up EHE reveals worrying evidence of inequality.

We must ensure that all perspectives are voiced so that EHE can be understood better. Policy makers, researchers and the vocal home education associations have had their say; now, attention needs to be paid to the voices of those at the centre of the debate. This chapter concludes with two examples of such research into EHE (Winstanley, 2009; Arora, 2002, 2006) to show that it is not just Gypsies and Travellers who take up EHE because of troubling issues in schools.

Home educating groups' experiences of EHE
'Too cool for school' *(Winstanley, 2009)*

Winstanley concentrates on the reasons families with highly able children, often labelled as 'gifted and talented', adopt home education.

> 'Gifted and talented' describes children and young people with an ability to develop to a level significantly ahead of their year group (or with the potential to develop those abilities): 'gifted' learners are those who are considered to have abilities in one or more academic subjects, like maths and English. 'Talented' learners are those who are considered to have practical skills in areas like sport, music, design or creative and performing arts.
>
> (DCSF, 2008)

Such children form a distinctive subset of the wider home education population, and their experiences would be familiar to Traveller children. Winstanley found that many of these children's families opt for EHE because of schools' inability to cope with their children. Gifted and talented children, like Travellers, are Othered in school, 'stereotyped and identified as different' (Kershen, 2011), and this has a profound impact on the support they receive.

Winstanley suggests other issues that also resonate with Travellers' difficulties in school. She says that mainstream schooling fails gifted and talented children because of its inflexible and exclusive structures. Her insightful paper shows how the issues and experiences of highly able children are very similar to those of Traveller children.

A further group of children Othered in mainstream education, who share similar experiences to both Traveller and gifted and talented children, are those pupils who have SEN; they were the focus of two studies by Arora. Before I discuss Arora's research it is helpful to reflect briefly upon the labels that are applied to children within the schooling system. Children are increasingly labelled according to their educational needs, talents, behaviour and even family income. The use of labels such as 'special educational needs' and 'gifted and talented' derive from a general condemnation by society of any characteristics that distinguish an individual from the norm (Fulcher and Scott, 2003). The problem with such labelling is that it draws attention to this special characteristic, which then becomes the central focus. Consequently, professionals may refer to the child only by the label, saying for example 'He is Special Needs'. Moreover, labelling can become a self-fulfilling prophecy, as teachers' expectations are constructed according to the assigned label rather than the individual child. However, the label can also initiate specialist support. I refer to children with SEN and gifted and talented children, not because I find the terms acceptable, but to illustrate the trend of educational experiences that come from being seen as different or the Other. These children, too, can be disadvantaged by unequal structures in school to the extent that their families feel they must withdraw them.

Elective home education and SEN (Arora, 2002–2006)

Arora's research (2002) on elective home education concerned the Yorkshire borough of Kirklees. She found that a large number of parents there withdrew their children from school due to concerns about inadequate academic support, bullying or other unhappy experiences at school. In her later paper on elective home education and special educational needs (2006), she noted that high numbers of parents of children with SEN statements were withdrawing them from school because their specific educational needs were not being met. Yet families did repeatedly try to make school work for them; 'it was only after a period of unhappiness and stress that they reluctantly started to home educate' (Arora, 2006: 59). Ofsted (2010) also reported that just over half the parents they surveyed were frustrated and upset by their children's experiences in school.

The literature suggests that school failure to include and support the most vulnerable groups of children often results in their moving to EHE, yet the EHE system leaves parents alone to cope with this situation. Arora

(2006) proposes that LAs should retain some responsibility for advice, resources and monitoring as part of a more flexible education plan. She recommends that when parents are considering EHE more support should be provided to allow various educational alternatives to be fully explored.

Both Winstanley's (2009) and Arora's (2002, 2006) research provides detail about why families opt for EHE, revealing important educational and equality issues. Arora (2006), Winstanley (2009), Webb (2010), Ivatts (2006) and Bhopal and Myers (2009a), and even Ofsted's own (2010a) research, indicate a connection between the choice of EHE and what is happening in schools. All the literature indicates that, as Blacker (1981) suggested, a worrying number of parents are home educating in order to compensate for the failure of schools to provide for their child's education. This failure, it seems, is being excused by the child's difference, be it one of race, culture or learning ability, and it is this difference that excludes them from the curriculum.

Note

[1] 'Gauje' is the Romani word used by Travellers to describe non-Travellers. It is not a derogatory term.

Chapter 6

Critical Race Theory, education and Travellers

> I think if they paid more attention, as much attention to Traveller children as other children, then I don't think there would be so much of a problem ... but where you have a Traveller child and an other child in a fight, then the Traveller child is always to blame. When you are in school you can always see the Traveller child falling behind and other child ain't ... I don't think they pay Traveller kids as much attention as they should pay them.

> It's the bullying as well; they say it does not happen but it do happen. Ronnie when he was in school he was being told he was eating hedgehogs. My children would not know what it was like to eat a hedgehog. On about eating rabbits, calling them Stinky Pikeys, well ... I had that when I was in school and it is still going on today so I know what the children are going through. We went through it when we was little.

> (Tina)

We hear stories every day on television, the Internet and in newspapers, from friends and families about their daily lives. We need stories to make sense of the world. Some are more convincing than others; some we never hear. Some, like the one above, we hear only if they are sought out, documented and shared. Critical race theorists use the power of stories and counter-stories to understand race and racism better, examining existing literature to highlight negative stories that perpetuate stereotypical thinking about certain minority ethnic groups and cultures. I use a combination of Gypsies' and other Travellers' stories and existing literature to tell an important story about educational inequality.

In this chapter, I discuss Critical Race Theory (CRT) and explore how it applies to Travellers and home education. I then use it to highlight and address important educational inequalities.

Critical Race Theory

Consider the events that happen most days within a school classroom. A Year Five pupil puts their hand up time after time but the teacher does not see or respond. Are other things happening in the classroom to distract the teacher? Is this just the way things are? Should we question such behaviour? The view we take is likely to be different depending on our own experiences and how we are treated by other people. Tina describes her children's experiences of such behaviour:

> One thing I get fed up with is when my children put their hands up and the teacher never says to them 'Right, you what is the question?' They sit there for 20 minutes and the teacher never asks them. Then they say to you that they never have their hand up and then you get your kids breaking down in tears in front of the teacher ... 'But I did have my hand up, you did not ask me anything'.
>
> (Tina)

Delgado and Stefancic are critical race scholars who criticize everyday classroom behaviours that are unjust. They say that, like water dripping on sandstone, such incidents as Tina describes are 'small acts of racism' (Delgado and Stefancic, 2001: 2). They may be consciously or unconsciously acted out, but they come from assumptions and stereotypes about certain people and communities in wider society. They affect behaviours and attitudes. They impact upon Traveller pupils' educational experiences. Because school represents a microcosm of wider society, issues of racism and discrimination are found there too. CRT scholars acknowledge that tackling inequality in schools is part of a wider battle.

Critical Race Theory developed from American legal studies in the 1970s. Lawyers, activists and legal scholars realized that progress in civil rights had stopped and there was danger of its reversing, so they continued the work towards the elimination of racism (Delgado and Stefancic, 2001; Matsuda *et al.*, 1993). Since this time CRT has expanded and is used with reference to law, sociology, history, education and women's studies (Solorzano and Yosso, 2002; Smith-Maddox and Solorzano, 2002). CRT theorists agree that to properly understand the complexities of race and racism it is important to draw on and work with various academic disciplines.

Ladson-Billings and Tate (2006) were the first to apply CRT to education. As Housee observes, CRT offers a framework to understand educational inequalities for different ethnic minority groups and to question their achievement, assessment structures, the content of the school curriculum and school exclusion:

> CRT in education examines not only the macro picture of policies, strategies, programmes and related practice across the entire educational endeavour, but also focuses on the micro picture of interpersonal behaviour, classroom interaction, participation and related outcomes.
>
> (Housee, 2012: 104)

Although commitments to equal opportunities are expressed in education policies, racism remains a significant and influential factor in certain ethnic minority groups' educational outcomes (Dixson and Rousseau, 2005). CRT scholars therefore critique such policies. They point out that the language on equal opportunity ignores past and continuing inequalities that continue to disadvantage minority groups:

> Critical race theorists view mainstream education as one of the many institutions that both historically and contemporarily serve to reproduce unequal power relations and academic outcomes.
>
> (Zamudio *et al.*, 2011: 4)

In the United Kingdom CRT is a focal point for work on race and is applied frequently to education. Gillborn (2005) suggests that CRT is useful for analysing UK education systems and structures because it recognizes the complicated and deeply embedded nature of racism. Gillborn uses CRT extremely effectively to scrutinize educational policies, academic selection and underachievement, and is one of the leading CRT scholars in the UK.

CRT is academic but at the same time practical. It is about raising critical questions and about challenging hidden operations of power that disadvantage many minority ethnic groups (Gillborn, 2008). CRT is not simply about producing new knowledge; it is essentially about critically informed action or praxis. The aim of CRT work is to achieve equitable and socially just relations of power (Ladson-Billings, 2009).

CRT is constantly developing. It is fluid. Like the British anti-racism movement as a whole, 'there is no single, unchanging statement of what CRT believes or suggests' (Gillborn, 2006: 251). Its fluidity mirrors the character of racism, multifaceted and ever-changing. However, CRT is underpinned by important principles:

- First, that racism is commonplace in society, legally, economically and socially.
- Second, that the focus must be on lived oppression – listening to the voices of the oppressed and problematizing dominant ideas in which knowledge is constructed.
- Third, a commitment to an interdisciplinary approach across fields of study.
- Fourth, a commitment to social justice through praxis (Solorzano, 1997, 1998).

Although many CRT scholars may refer to 'people of colour' they are describing all minority groups; for this reason I argue that CRT is relevant in thinking about inequalities in education for Gypsy and other Traveller children. CRT links racism and discrimination in society to education. This can help us understand educational segregation and other equality issues that Gypsy and Traveller pupils experience. Showman communities are not legally defined as an ethnic minority group, and are in many ways very different from ethnic minority Traveller groups; still, in this book I apply CRT to highlight racism towards all Traveller groups. This is a connection that has not been made before within Gypsy and Traveller literature and making it may contribute to the development of a new dimension within CRT. The principles of CRT apply to Travellers and education.

The centrality of racism

CRT concentrates on the continuing and embedded existence of racism. As Justice Harry Blackmun in 1978 said: 'In order to get beyond racism, we must first take account of race. There is no other way' ('Blackmun, H.', 2006).

CRT scholars argue that racism is not always obvious. They draw attention to racism's normalized place in society and education and 'its routine (often unrecognized) character' (Gillborn, 2008: 27). The use of language and the law with reference to Travellers provides good examples. To return to the quote from Tina:

> Ronnie when he was in school he was being told he was eating hedgehogs. My children would not know what it was like to eat a hedgehog. On about eating rabbits, calling them 'Stinky Pikey'...
>
> (Tina)

The words used to insult Ronnie demonstrate how Gypsy and Traveller people are defined as Other. Racism is rooted in such language. Others are stereotyped according to a set of negative descriptions that apparently justify their exclusion from full participation in society (Devine *et al.*, 2008). Now consider the relationship between the state and Gypsy and Traveller communities. Laws passed over the years have effectively forbidden and problematized all Travellers' ways of life (Foster and Norton, 2012). Currently, few demands are made on local authorities to provide Gypsy and other Traveller sites, but this was not always the case. The 1968 Caravan Sites Act required LAs to provide for the accommodation needs of all Travellers and funding was available to do so. This Act was abolished in 1994, creating a shortage of appropriate accommodation and stopping-places for mobile and settled Gypsies and other Travellers across the UK. Settled society seems to expect Traveller people to live in houses (Morris and Clements, 1999). The case of Dale Farm, a large Irish Traveller site (where almost half the residents were living without agreed planning permission), exposed how willing LAs are to spend millions on evicting families.

In January 2013, the government suggested removing section 444(6) of the Education Act 1996, which supports Gypsy and Traveller families who are highly mobile. Legally this section ensures that, if travelling for work purposes, Traveller parents will not be penalized for their children's non-attendance at school, as long as this does not exceed 100 days in one academic year. Although the consultation on the proposal to drop this section was called 'improving educational outcomes for children of travelling families', its content suggests the opposite agenda. Showman and Fairground communities, schools and various Traveller organizations have opposed the section's removal. Debates within the House of Commons mirror their concerns for highly mobile Travellers such as Showmen, as in this quote from the conservative Member of Parliament for Gloucester, Richard Graham:

> [T]he consequences of any proposed changes to legislation must ensure that they do not unintentionally damage the fabric of life of some 24,000 people; and that the government's drive to improve exam results is not at the cost of close-knit, resilient and independent families.
>
> (United Kingdom, House of Commons, 18 June 2013)

Legal frameworks and policies often act against minority groups. It took until 2011 for the national census to include Gypsy, Roma and Irish Traveller communities as distinct ethnic groups, even though various Traveller groups have been living in the UK since at least the 1500s. Continually depicting Travellers as Other has fostered racism towards all Traveller groups and communities, who continue to be the subject of openly-expressed racist views (Willers, 2012).

In 2003 a MORI poll reported that 35 per cent of the UK population admitted to prejudice against Gypsies and Travellers (Stonewall, 2003). Over a third of all respondents cited newspapers and television as the major influence on their views of Gypsies and Travellers. As the CRE observed, 'Extreme levels of public hostility ... [are] fuelled in part by irresponsible media reporting of the kind that would be met with outrage if it was targeted at any other ethnic group' (CRE, 2003). A study concentrating on interviews with professional police officers (Coxhead, 2007) found that prejudice towards Travellers was ingrained in the police force.

Responses informed by CRT, in recognizing that issues of racism are central in addressing social and educational inequalities, can prompt defensive reactions. Hylton suggests that CRT allows you to draw from scholars who are not afraid of making bold statements and challenging the racialized order of things (Hylton, 2012: 25). However, CRT also recognizes that 'racism' is a highly contested and provocative term. It sounds unforgiving, so people often respond defensively to any suggestion that they might be racist (Gillborn, 2008). My professional experience bears this out. Racist remarks or behaviours that I challenged were often excused or simply ignored by those around me, and little progress was made in improving attitudes towards Gypsies and other Travellers.

A focus on lived oppression

CRT emerged out of the need for a new vocabulary, one that could name racism and address race-related structures of oppression in a better way. CRT scholars use critical White Studies to raise challenging questions and analyse what it means to be and not be White (Gillborn, 2006). These studies are not an assault on White people but they do represent an assault on the social construction and persistently reinforced power of White identities and interests (Gillborn, 2008), since White power and advantage can secure the right to exclude others. An example in relation to Travellers' education is found in eastern Europe, where for generations many Roma children have been placed automatically into segregated or special schools for the 'mentally disabled' (Equality and the Roma Education Fund, 2011; Wilkin *et al.*, 2009). Even where Roma are educated in mainstream schools they are often separated from the other children on grounds of their cultural differences (European Commission, 2004).

In England, a subtler variant of such segregation is found. Gypsy and other Traveller children are often classified as low achievers and inappropriately labelled as having SEN (Wilkin *et al.*, 2009). They are therefore, like Roma in mainland Europe, segregated by achievement and labelled as having SEN on the basis of their cultural difference. Here we see evidence of the way in which assumptions about race and cultural differences single out the Traveller child as deficient. This is not an issue for Traveller communities alone, however. Observe an interesting parallel with DePouw's (2012) work on Hmong American students:

> Majority explanations of inequities in Hmong American education often describe Hmong American student and family experiences in terms of 'culture clash' or profound cultural differences thereby obscuring the ways in which Hmong Americans have been racialized as refugees, Southeast Asians and as 'Blackened' and gendered low income communities of color.
>
> (DePouw, 2012: 223)

CRT provides a 'critical lens' and an appropriate language to analyse, understand and disseminate knowledge about such inequalities (Dixson and Rousseau, 2005). It also offers various methods and tools for moving forward from theory to educational action. One method, Critical White Studies, has been noted. Storytelling, counter-stories and interest convergence are further useful methods, which I draw upon and discuss shortly. I now examine the concept and relevance of Whiteness for Travellers and education.

How Whiteness works

Whiteness is a system of beliefs and privileges, although it does not map automatically onto skin tone (Gillborn, 2010). Many Travellers in England are white-skinned, although this varies from family to family, whereas Roma communities in the UK tend to have darker skin. However, there is ample evidence of racism and marginalization in society towards all Travellers, whether they are Gypsies, Roma, Showmen or Travellers of Irish heritage. All Traveller groups are categorized as being outside the majority culture. In the political and sociological sense that CRT uses the word Whiteness, all Travellers are therefore a minoritized racial Other. In the context of CRT they are not White (Gillborn, personal communication, 9 November 2011). Like other Black minority groups they experience inequality, but the fact that many Travellers in England have pale skin means they can easily 'pass' or 'play White' (Derrington, 2007). This reality can be problematic when trying to address racism as it complicates analysis of what is nonetheless racist discrimination.

Some minority groups have 'become White', although CRT scholars argue that this happens only when it serves White self-interest, when there is 'interest convergence'. Take, for example, Irish people who went to the USA in the 1800s to escape racial oppression and religious persecution in their own country (Takiki, 1993). When they arrived they were regarded as working class and as socially closer to Blacks than Whites (Leonardo, 2002). But when competition for employment increased, the White bourgeoisie sought to disrupt existing Irish and Black partnerships to preserve their own power. So they gave Irish immigrants opportunities to join them socially, to become 'White', and thus maintained White superiority. The Irish people welcomed this opportunity, because it secured their social mobility and economic independence (Leonardo, 2002), but it arose only when it was in the White majority's interest. The importance of power relations in enabling social inclusion and promoting the equality of marginalized groups is laid bare in such cases; governments and political figures will use extreme measures to achieve their political and economic objectives (Davis, 2008: 13).

Though many governments use policy in their efforts to address inequality, CRT scholars argue that policy alone is not enough. In England the Race Relations Amendment Act (2000) placed new duties on public bodies, including schools, to address institutional racism. Gillborn (2006) rightly states that although the language may since have changed, the reality of race inequality has not. Many Gypsy and other Traveller children still 'play White' in order to survive in school (Derrington, 2007). For Travellers to become White in the CRT sense, the dominant majority must encourage this process. The evidence of both obvious and hidden structures of racism towards all Traveller communities highlights the majority's lack of interest in doing so. This curtails Gypsies' and Travellers' social power and agency and impedes their children's educational opportunities.

The importance of experiential knowledge: Storytelling and counter-stories

One of the greatest contributions of CRT is its emphasis on narratives and counter stories told from the vantage point of the oppressed. Critical race theorists engage in the practice of retelling history from a minority perspective. In doing so, CRT exposes the contradictions inherent in the dominant storyline that among other things blames minority groups of people for their own condition of inequality. Critical race theorists understand that narratives are not neutral but rather political expressions

> of power relationships. That is, history is always told from the perspective of the dominant group. Minority perspectives in the form of narratives, testimonies, or storytelling challenge the dominant groups' accepted truths.
>
> (Zamudio *et al.*, 2011: 5)

Critical race scholars document the voices of marginalized communities and individuals to share their lived experiences of racism and inequalities. They profess the experiential knowledge of marginalized communities as legitimate, appropriate and necessary to understanding education. The notion of voice is used to assert the experiential knowledge of minority people and their communities (Ladson-Billings, 2009). Documenting Travellers' own accounts adds their voices to the educational debate and can disrupt commonly held stereotypes or mistaken assumptions about Travellers' educational needs and wishes.

In Bhopal and Myers's (2009a) research into Travellers' use of EHE, the professionals they interviewed spoke of the problems of bullying, name-calling and lack of understanding for Traveller cultures in school. But they all stressed that the highly mobile nature of Traveller families was the key reason for their uptake of EHE. Professionals assumed that Traveller families were moving around, but (as we saw in Chapter 5) mobility was not a reason that any of the Traveller families interviewed gave for choosing EHE, and not one of them lived mobile lives at the time. Were the professionals ill-informed? Were they relying on cultural stereotypes to explain away Travellers' reasons for home educating? These questions are why it is so important to locate and share Travellers' stories, so we can provide counter-stories that expose, analyse and challenge common stereotypes and assumptions about minority groups.

A counter-story challenges or counteracts the dominant story (Dixson and Rousseau, 2005). It is, as Solorzano and Yosso (2002) observe, a method for telling the stories of those whose experiences often go untold. Stovall (2006) suggests counter-stories are essential; in education, they disrupt the dominant stories, which depict minority communities as anti-school or anti-intellectual. Counter-stories can redirect our viewpoint and enable us to see in new ways. They illuminate fresh perspectives and can facilitate a better understanding of education. They reveal inequality by 'turning up the volume on the depressed or inaudible voice' (Clough, 2002: 67). Listening to such voices raises important questions about educational structures, policies and practices.

Solorzano and Yosso (2002) created counter-stories by combining research data, the existing literature on the topics and their professional and personal experiences. Here I take a similar approach, with particular emphasis on documenting Gypsies' and other Travellers' personal accounts of EHE and education. I use the information gathered to challenge the literature that depicts all Travellers in a negative light. The theme of *voice* runs through this account.

The use of an interdisciplinary approach

CRT is interdisciplinary and activist. It insists upon critical race work that recognizes the complexity of discrimination and is part of a broader movement towards social justice (Stovall, 2006; DePouw, 2012). CRT brings together the literature on law, history, sociology and education to better understand the effects of racism, sexism and classism on marginalized groups (Solorzano and Yosso, 2002). In England some policies already encourage an interdisciplinary approach, but further actions are needed to address racism. The Macpherson Report (1999), which investigated racist issues surrounding the murder of the black teenager Stephen Lawrence, recommended that in order to eradicate racism 'specific and co-ordinated action' was required, both within agencies and society, and 'particularly through the education system' (Macpherson, 1999: para.6.54, p.33).

Inequality is not about race alone; it is made up of different 'layers of subordination' (Solorzano and Yosso, 2002; Phoenix, 2009). Individual Traveller children may experience inequality on grounds of their race, gender, social class and cultural group; CRT recognizes that such multidimensional inequalities exist. As Collins *et al.* (2000: 42) point out, 'cultural patterns of oppression are not only interrelated but are bound together and influenced by the intersectional systems of society'. The concept of intersectionality refers to the ways in which 'the variables of diversity interact and interrelate' ('Intersectionality', 2012: xlix). The term intersectionality captures the multiple ways in which structures of privilege and disadvantage intersect in people's lives, reminding us that discrimination is not necessarily about one issue but rather reflects a matrix of intersecting inequalities. Critical race scholars (Solorzano and Yosso, 2002; Stovall, 2006: Gillborn, 2006; DePouw, 2012) thus approach the study of race and racism in increasingly complex ways. They draw attention to the intersection of inequalities that minority groups experience on account of racism, culture, ethnicity, class, gender, sexuality and other differences.

There are limitations to analysing intersecting inequalities together: the process and findings may be overly complex and can dilute the focus on race equality. CRT recognizes this challenge and places racism centre-stage, while also considering other inequalities as they can and do affect people's experiences of education and society more generally. Observing race as the only disadvantage for Gypsy and other Travellers would certainly be a limiting proposition. Intersectionality is relevant to all Travellers' educational experiences. Their position as an Other is underpinned by complex and intersecting inequalities that increase their disadvantage on different levels.

The concept of intersectionality can be a valuable analytical tool in tracing how certain groups are situated as not just different but deviant (Staunaes, 2003). Teranishi (2002) uses CRT as a lens to examine, for example, the intersections of ethnicity, social class and immigration among Asian Pacific Americans, problematizing more traditional theories that focus on race alone. CRT, then, is committed to an interdisciplinary and cross-cutting analysis of inequality. Scholars use the CRT framework to illuminate the complex nature of racism and other forms of exclusion (Gillborn, 2008), but they also use it to do more: to propose radical solutions to address this racism (Ladson-Billings, 2009: 33).

The commitment to social justice

CRT scholarship can provide a creative, pragmatic approach that challenges racism and discrimination and works towards ending oppression (Matsuda *et al.*, 1993; Stovall, 2006). CRT is underpinned by basic insights and specific conceptual tools. Many scholars use a range of CRT tenets and tools to critique and challenge racism and other oppressions. Housee, for instance uses CRT as a tool to unpack Islamophobia in her teaching (2012). She examines debates on Islamophobia in her own classroom and compares her students' experiences with the policies and ideals that reinforce racism. She uses CRT to inform anti-racist teaching – that is, she takes political action.

Another creative example can be seen in Rollock's (2012) work on the invisibility of race. As a Black academic she uses autobiography, data analysis and counter-narrative to interrogate the norms and practices of educational spaces. She documents the educational strategies of members of the Black middle classes, using her own voice alongside parents' accounts to highlight 'the pervasiveness of the racial power dynamics at play across the education system as a whole' (Rollock, 2012: 67).

This chapter began by telling part of Tina's story. She felt that her kids were paid no attention in school; that they tried to participate in lessons but were ignored. They were called 'Stinky Pikey' and told they ate hedgehogs. Having experienced racist language and indifference to her educational needs when she was a child, she wanted better for her children. So she withdrew them from school. At home they are not bullied, but they are missing out on their right to an education at school through no fault of their own.

Conclusion

In all societies and cultures, people tell stories. Listening to stories can help us to understand not only personal lives but also local and national issues. CRT uses stories to understand and act on racism and inequalities and offers a theoretical framework within which to study the challenges within Traveller education.

- CRT acknowledges overt racism and, perhaps more crucially, addresses the subtleties of hidden racism and the cultural Otherness of Traveller groups within education. These subtleties, which portray Travellers as different and deviant, are potentially more destructive than overt racism because they are an ingrained and invisible day-to-day feature of Travellers' lives (Carmichael and Hamilton, 2001).
- CRT provides a critical lens through which we can reconsider policy and practice and helps us reassess everyday language and behaviours.
- CRT makes us take a second look at any situation, and this can lead to a better understanding of education and how to make it fairer.
- CRT has the advantage of being infinitely flexible: scholars can draw creatively upon its tenets and tools. In this book I use storytelling and counter-stories to develop understanding about inequality. The concept of interest convergence is used to reveal the subtle, covert and yet persistent aspects of racism that perpetuate minority groups' social exclusion. Educational exclusion on racist grounds remains a real issue for all Traveller families.

The chapter began by reflecting on the importance of locating, collecting and sharing stories. In the next chapter, I consider how such research can be undertaken ethically and with respect for the people involved, particularly when they belong to marginalized groups.

Chapter 7
Undertaking research with marginalized groups

> When we think about what we are doing as researchers, one of our main tasks is to acquire knowledge. For some researchers their task begins and ends there.
>
> (Cram, 1992: 28)

Research can be thought of as a purely academic and objective process. But if you are undertaking educational or social research with people then it is unethical to centre the research solely on acquiring new knowledge. Research generally still assumes that the researcher is the sole producer of new knowledge, but this assumption silences the people who are the subject of the study and ignores their personal knowledge (Pizarro, 1999). This approach is disrespectful, unfair and also incomplete. In this chapter, I discuss ways of undertaking research: how to collect, analyse and share findings in a way that ensures research participants are respected and their voices are heard. The focus is on research with Gypsies and other Travellers but illustrates good practice in research involving any individual or group.

The skills used in research are not purely academic either. Research is part of our daily activities at home and work. In deciding where we will go on holiday, we investigate different locations and venues and consider the travel options. We research the best options so that we can come to an informed decision. In the workplace we might present the available evidence to undertake a specific piece of work, or to demonstrate success in completing a project. Whether we are collecting feedback from customers in the workplace or budgeting our own holiday costs we are using research skills. Research can be described as a disciplined, balanced enquiry, conducted in a critical spirit (Thomas, 2009). Research is important because it:

- produces new knowledge;
- allows us to investigate matters about which we may know little;
- provides evidence to inform practice or policy;
- improves understanding of a specific subject;
- is a way of evidencing concerns about issues that need to be addressed.

Collecting data
Ethics
Data collection is the procedure through which different data sources are produced and brought together (Grix, 2004). There is clear guidance on undertaking data collection as part of educational research. The British Educational Research Association (BERA) booklet offers ethical guidelines and recognizes the researcher's ethical responsibility with regard to those people under study (BERA, 2011). There are ethical concerns around the conduct of research practice and respect for others (Thomas, 2009). As each piece of research is unique, standard guidance may not be enough on its own to prevent harm; therefore, 'every research project needs to be considered in its own right' (Sikes, 2007: 16). The researcher can be advised, but will also need to take responsibility for considering the particulars of their own study.

It is useful to look at other researchers' approaches. Smith (1999) highlights how in New Zealand ethical standards for research with Maori communities extend 'far beyond issues of individual consent and confidentiality' (Smith, 1999: 119). Ngahuia Te Awekotuku (1991) has identified a set of ethical guidelines pointing out the responsibilities researchers owe to Maori people. I suggest that these guidelines are appropriate for undertaking research with any marginalized group:

1. *Aroha ki te tangata* (have a basic respect for people)
2. *Kanohi kitea* (the seen face: that is, present yourself to people face to face)
3. *Titiro, whakarongo … korero* (look, listen … speak)
4. *Manaaki ki te tangata* (share and host people; be generous)
5. *Kia tupato* (be cautious)
6. *Kaua e takahia te mana o te tangata* (do not trample on the mana of people)
7. *Kaua e mahaki* (don't flaunt your knowledge)

(Smith, 1999: 120)

Respect
Researchers should take care not to exploit the very people they want to involve in their research. In the past, research has unfortunately been used to take advantage of marginalized groups in society, a trend that has left a legacy. Aboriginal people have been used and oppressed through research. Smith explains that:

> the term 'research' itself is inextricably linked to European imperialism and colonialism. The word itself 'research' is probably one of the dirtiest words in the indigenous world's vocabulary ... Just knowing that someone measured our faculties by filling the skulls of our ancestors with millet seeds and compared the amount of millet seed to the capacity for mental thought offends our sense of who and what we are.
>
> (Smith, 1999: 1)

Early researchers seemed to be fascinated with perceived differences between people. Research was used to measure differences between different 'races'. In the nineteenth century, anthropologists studying African, Asian, Native American and Australasian communities undertook measurements of skull size and weight and, as Smith (above) observed, used this research to make claims about intelligence and to 'prove' European peoples' supremacy. Historically, research has also been used to inflict sterilization on disabled people or those with mental health issues. Children have been forcibly removed from indigenous families. Little wonder, then, that we need to think carefully about the effects of research on its subjects:

> The term 'respect' is consistently used by indigenous peoples to underscore the significance of our relationships and humanity. Through respect the place of everyone and everything in the universe is kept in balance and harmony. Respect is a reciprocal, shared, and constantly interchanging principle which is expressed through all aspects of social conduct.
>
> (Smith, 1999: 120)

To conduct my own work respectfully, I chose data collection methods that draw on Gypsies' and Travellers' own practices and emphasize their voices. There is a strong oral tradition of communication within Gypsy and Traveller communities, so I decided that interviews were an appropriate way to collect data about their home educating experiences. The interviews could support interactive research and capture participants' precise meanings and worldviews (Kvale and Brinkman, 2009). Moreover, the advantage of the interview process is that it allowed me to attend to Gypsies' and Travellers' own voices.

My review of previous research on EHE (Ivatts, 2006; Ofsted, 2010; see Chapter 6 in this volume) highlighted the limitations of methods such as questionnaires. Most pertinently, questionnaires are restrictive in that they do not require face-to-face interaction with research participants, meaning responses may be limited and respondents may understand questions in a different way than that intended by the researcher (Walker, 1985). Due to the low literacy levels within the adult Gypsy and Traveller population (EHRC, 2010) and their frequently geographically isolated living arrangements, I felt that questionnaires would not provide high-quality data. For one thing, if posted, they might not reach the homes of respondents – I had found that letters to Gypsy and Traveller families were often lost due to complex or inaccurate postcodes on sites. Moreover, a questionnaire format would not invite rich descriptions of individuals' experiences and views.

Presenting yourself to people face to face

Before any data collection can begin the researcher must obtain informed consent, defined by Diener and Crandall (1978) as the procedure by which individuals choose whether or not to participate in a research project after being informed of all the facts likely to influence their decision. The principle of informed consent derives from the subjects' right to freedom and autonomy. Consent protects and respects the right of autonomy, recognizing participants' right to refuse to participate and to withdraw at any point (Frankfort-Nachmais and Nachmais, 1992).

Burman (1994) states that researchers should be as open as possible about their aims, to ensure that research participants are provided with all the information they need. I wanted to ensure that my research participants could understand this information and make informed decisions about their participation. I was particularly aware of some families' low literacy levels and knew that the Gypsy and other Traveller families I spoke to would need much more than an information letter to consent to the research. I approached the families myself so I could explain my research information letter in detail and ask for their participation. I asked those who agreed to participate to sign a consent form, and gave them a copy of it. Although I was able to meet most families face to face to ask for informed consent, there were two families I had to telephone and interestingly, they both declined, suggesting that face to face communication may be the best way to establish trust in a sensitive research area.

Being cautious

Large numbers of Gypsies and other Travellers reside across the county of Saltfield. The main groups are English Romany Gypsies, Travellers of Irish heritage and Showmen. Travellers of Irish heritage and Showmen are highly mobile and move in and out of the county, whereas the Romany Gypsy families are more settled. Travellers' socio-economic situations are also diverse, ranging from very poor to affluent.

I decided very carefully who would participate in the research. I wanted to make sure that the families I interviewed had registered for EHE and represented the characteristics of the Gypsies and Travellers living in Saltfield. No Irish Travellers were registered, and I did not include such families in my research. Neither did I include families who were not registered formally as providing EHE, although this would be a further research study of interest, as many Traveller children are not registered in any educational provision.

My sampling of research participants was designed to reflect relevant geographical locations, a range of travelling patterns, a range of socio-economic statuses and a range of Traveller groups. A quota selection of this kind identifies major subgroups and then selects a number of participants from each (see Miles and Huberman, 1994), producing a sample range of informants that represents the overall group and can thus support the credibility of the research (Shenton, 2004).

Nelson (2011) points out that research in the field of home education is often conducted by insiders – that is, by people who are home educated themselves. This is a potential concern, along with the number of voluntary, self-selected samples, as it may produce bias. Arora (2002, 2006) notes that the self-selecting nature of the participants in EHE studies is the main criticism of the field, since self-selecting participants may be more highly motivated and better educated than the home educating group overall, and their children may thus be at an advantage. Recruiting voluntary research participants alone does not ensure a representative sample, since it leaves the researcher considering only the views of those who came forward – those more likely to be positive about the results. Gabb (2004) suggests that this puts us in the position of a researcher who studies gambling but considers only the opinions of the winners: we only hear from those who come forward to talk about their prize.

For both ethical and practical reasons, I concentrated on interviewing family units rather than individual parents or children. Families could themselves select who took part in the interview; parents were present at all times and children could take part if the family wished. Many family units had more than one child being home educated; across the 11 families involved there were 42 children, 32 of whom were being, or had been, home educated. Fifteen children in these 11 families were currently being home educated. The other 10 children were in education, of pre-school age or old enough to work.

Children were present at many interviews and contributed sporadically, depending on their age and interest. The mother generally led in the interviews and the children spoke up as and when they liked. In a few situations the young Travellers themselves led in the interviews because their families considered their views to be important. But other family members were present and contributed when they wished. No fathers involved themselves in the interviews, although they were often around in the background, getting on with other things. In two cases grandmothers were part of the family group.

Not trampling on the mana of people or flaunting your knowledge

Being careful about your research approach can ensure that participants feel included and valued. Most interviews took place in the families' homes, as this was the setting where home education took place. I believed that holding interviews in an office or away from the Travellers' homes would reduce participation, as families had children to care for and jobs to get on with. The participants seemed comfortable and relaxed in their own environment. I wore casual clothing and conducted the interviews as conversations, using questions to focus discussion. Burman (1994) suggests that, while the interview schedule is reassuring for the researcher because it concerns the issues the researcher wants to discuss, flexibility is needed to ensure that participants are not intimidated and do not fail to follow the researcher's objectives. I followed Clough and Nutbrown (2007), allowing my schedule to guide rather than direct the interviews.

I wanted to use the interviews to capture the voices of Gypsies and other Travellers and to assert their knowledge, not to flaunt my own. Clough and Nutbrown (2007) advise that audio and video recordings are by far the best way to obtain interview data, as relying on hand-written notes means inevitably that some comments are lost. With the permission of all participants, the interviews were recorded on a digital recorder. I planned to make notes throughout each interview but found this was both intimidating and distracting for participants and hindered the flow of discussion. I therefore relied heavily on the digital recorder, which twice let me down due to data overload and batteries running down. This is the kind of incident that you seldom hear about. Losing two whole interviews can be quite devastating!

In one case I had no choice but to handwrite notes because the respondent wanted to be interviewed at her place of work and it was impossibly noisy. Although hand-written notes did limit data collection in this particular case, I held a second interview meeting to extend these notes. Research can be messy and unpredictable, but the difficulties are often the things you learn most from: 'Educational research is without doubt a messy business and it would be wrong to pretend otherwise' (Wellington, 2000).

Educational research aims to extend knowledge and understanding in all areas of educational activity and from all perspectives, including those of learners, educators, policymakers and the public (BERA, 2011). The complexities and challenges of undertaking educational research are seldom discussed. Journal articles may report briefly on methodology and methods but they rarely offer critical discussions of the reality and ethical considerations of the research process itself. More discussions on such matters would be informative for anyone undertaking or wanting to undertake research.

Analysing the data

Data analysis is an integral part of the research process. Wellington (2000) observes that the quality of the research project does not necessarily derive from the quality or quantity of the data collected; what matters is the interpretation of this data and the connections made with existing theoretical models. There are many ways to analyse the data you collect and there are many publications on different analytical processes. Rather than suggesting any particular process, I reflect on how we can work with research participants to ensure their engagement and make sure it is their voices that are documented and not our own.

Voice

Although voice has many meanings in research (Guba and Lincoln, 2005), the description I favour can be expressed as a political and moral response to the inequality faced by oppressed and silenced minority groups (Nutbrown and Hannon, 2003).

I made a deliberate choice to focus on Gypsies and Travellers' voices. I drew on Travellers' own words to describe their experiences, and these are documented throughout this book. To omit the voices of those who experience EHE systems first-hand and who play such a vital part in my research would have been unjust. I chose not to document the views of teachers and other educators because these have already been documented in other research on Travellers and EHE (Ivatts, 2006). Their stories form part of the master narrative that portrays Travellers in a negative light.

I recognize that I am in a more privileged position than other researchers, as I had access to Gypsy and Traveller families through my professional working practice. In some ways I could be considered an insider in the community as I have worked alongside many Traveller families. My experience has enabled me to understand Travellers' situations and what they say in a way that no newcomer could (Reinhartz, 1992). But I am also a Gorja or Gauje and clearly not an insider or member of the community. In their research with Traveller students in secondary schools, Derrington and Kendall (2004) noted that the fact that they, the researchers, were not Travellers was bound to influence responses and that some of the responses were likely to be influenced by the unnatural experience of being interviewed by a Gauje. The same was true in my research. I was conscious that my study demanded a lot from families because I asked them to cross personal boundaries and share private family practices and thoughts with someone who is not a Traveller and who worked for an LA.

One participant, Tina, was very sceptical about what the outcome of her interview with me would be, and gave her opinion of previous consultations: 'You never hear anything else about it and if they do come around they say it's no further forward!' I could not promise that my research would change the discrimination her children had experienced in school and which made her withdraw them for EHE. This interview reflected the frustrations and the problems that Gypsies and other Travellers experience in education and with consultation, especially when speaking to educators or researchers produced little response or improvement. It is important to document these difficulties because research is not always straightforward.

Listening to and documenting the voices of the marginalized requires important ethical considerations. I was mindful of the power hierarchy that can exist between the researcher and the researched. Tierney's (1995) and Liebrow's (1993) work on the issue of voice and the relationship constructed with individuals under study is insightful. Liebrow (1993) openly shared his research process and views with his homeless interviewees, telling those with whom he worked about his own opinions of the issues involved and discussing ways to improve the situation.

I followed similar procedures in my research by explaining to respondents the research aims, process and possible consequences of their involvement. I also shared my research findings when I revisited families for the second interview. Tierney (1995) emphasizes that researchers should present their work so that it is accessible and enables the reader to observe the voices of those interviewed. The sharing of research is an ethical consideration.

Sharing the research

Shenton (2004) recommends that researchers should provide a full description of the process and product of their research so that readers can understand and assess it and its value. Before we share research, though, we must ensure it is trustworthy and reliable. Presenting unreliable or unfounded research is disrespectful and can harm people, as historical examples of the use of research have shown.

Validity

There is much discussion about the validity of research. The field of validity is concerned with identifying measures that lead to credible conclusions and assessing the degree to which the methods used accurately measure what they claim to (Wellington, 2000). This approach may be relevant when you are working with statistics but is not necessarily so when you undertake research with people. You cannot measure people or their circumstances. You cannot say whether they are right or wrong, because everyone has a different reality and interprets situations differently. Such research is subjective and often interpretative and qualitative.

An interpretative approach recognizes that research participants' views are diverse and plentiful. Interpretivism is a qualitative research approach (Cresswell, 2009: 8) that seeks to document participants' understandings of the situation being studied. Within this sort of research the idea that there exists one single reality or truth is questionable, even unthinkable (Sikes, 2007). For these reasons, interpretative researchers like Guba and Lincoln (1985) prefer not to use the term 'validity' but use phrases like trustworthiness instead, seeking to encourage researchers to persuade an audience that their findings are worth paying attention to.

In research focused on the views and voices of others these voices must speak out to the reader. Interviews can capture Gypsies' and other Travellers' voices, informing understandings about education and highlight issues of inequality. Such data is incontestable – the participants' words provide concrete, vivid and meaningful data, more convincing to readers than any researcher's opinion (Miles and Huberman, 1994). It is the voices of participants that should be documented, not those of the researcher.

Another way to ensure that research is ethical and respectful is to member-check your data – that is, to check your analytical categories, interpretations and conclusions with your participants. Guba and Lincoln (1985) name the member-check as the most crucial technique for establishing trustworthiness. It is right that research participants should confirm that what is written about them is accurate.

Neutrality

We need to recognize that we cannot be wholly neutral. As a researcher involved with people in a specific area of interest you are totally engaged, so you cannot possibly be entirely neutral. Be open and honest about your own position, stating it early on. That way, readers can tell where you are coming from.

My experiences of working with Gypsy and Traveller families and seeing racism and discrimination towards them at first hand influenced my choice of research approach and methods. As Clough and Nutbrown (2007) suggest, decisions about research often seem practical, yet they can carry deep, unarticulated values and beliefs. Overt racism towards Gypsies and other Travellers is still widely tolerated; in addition, subtle forms of racism are at work. The press, particularly red-top or tabloid newspapers – which often use sensational and populist content to target a mass readership, whereas broadsheets generally adopt a more thoughtful and reasoned approach (Foster and Norton, 2012) – perpetuates negative discourses concerning Gypsy and other Traveller communities. In my critical enquiry I wanted to highlight the consequences of overt racism and also examine the subtle institutional structures, attitudes and prejudices of this type that fuel the difficulties Gypsies and other Travellers experience in accessing and achieving in education.

Public dissemination

Public dissemination can take many forms. Research can be shared through academic papers and conferences, in articles, books or short reports. You may present your research to fellow students, your lecturer, other professionals or your friends. Tierney (1995) stresses that researchers need to share findings with the people studied and not make exaggerated claims about their research. Te Awekotuku and Maori (1991) warn that researchers must not trample over the mana of people and should not flaunt their knowledge; just so, we should take care when we present the findings of research. Research findings can be misquoted to the detriment of those under study and it is hard to prevent such misquoting from informing later reports. However, by sharing research findings with participants and ensuring that they are informed on and agree to proposed conclusions, you can at least ensure they know your intentions are worthy. There are various ways to ensure the research reaches those who have contributed, such as letting them have copies of audio tapes, DVDs, short articles with diagrams or publications in relevant languages to ensure that the participants can access and understand what you are doing.

Protection

Researchers have a responsibility to protect their participants' well-being. The research must be designed to protect their privacy, well-being and confidentiality. Do not document real names, addresses or details of the participants as this may expose them, but generalizations should be avoided where there is no evidence to substantiate them. I am cautious in reporting my findings on EHE and Traveller families as my research represents the views of only a small number of Romany Gypsies and Showmen families; I cannot claim that these will represent all Travellers' opinions.

Research involving people is messy and complex but it is important, particularly research that involves minority communities. Thinking about and planning the research properly, and talking with those you seek to involve from the start, can help ensure that no harm comes to them and shows that you are respectful. Properly conducted, research can empower people and communities and it can produce new knowledge. Sharing the findings can inform others of significant matters about which little is known. One of the ways to address inequality and discrimination is to ensure that people have the correct information. Research can give an insight into other people's lives and realities; it can assert the voices of the marginalized and change negative perceptions and attitudes.

Chapter 8

How Gypsy and Traveller families use EHE

> Critical Race Theory emphasizes narrative and counter stories told from the vantage point of the oppressed. Narratives are not neutral; they are political expressions of power relationships. History is always told from the perspective of the dominant group. Critical race theorists engage in the practice of retelling history from a minority perspective. They do this to expose contradictions and inaccuracies inherent within dominant storylines that blame minority groups for the conditions of inequality.
>
> (Zamudio *et al.*, 2011: 5)

I identify four important reasons for listening to Gypsies' and Travellers' own opinions about EHE:

- Not much is known by the dominant society about what they think.
- To tell the stories of Gypsies and Travellers, from their own, and not a White perspective.
- To show contradictions and challenge inaccuracies and stereotypical assumptions.
- To better understand educational provision.

Listening to other people's experiences of education can reveal things you have never considered. This is particularly important when considering issues of racism and inequality. The next two chapters look in detail at how 11 Traveller families use EHE. The number of children in each family ranged from 1 to 7, with an average of 4 per family. Out of the 42 children in all, 32 had been or were being home educated; 9 of the remaining siblings had attended or were still attending school and one was still a baby. The interviews concentrated mainly on the children who were currently being home educated, although families talked frequently about their other children's experiences of EHE and schooling.

    Remember that this may not be a typical sample of families. A list of pseudonyms is given below for all the people involved.

Table 8.1: Pseudonyms of Gypsy/Roma and Showman respondents

Parent/carer name	No. of children in family	Children referred to directly in study
Patricia	3	Marsha, David and Victoria
Elizabeth	3	Shannon, Nathan and Patricia
Jolene	4	Amos, Albie, Bobbie and Joe
Teresa	6	Bobby
Anona	1	Kelly
Tina	3	Ronnie and Davey
Anita	2	Tony and Libby
Marie	7	Rocky and Caprice
Vicky	6	Crystal and Alfie
Vanessa	3	Courtney
Carol-Anne	4	Roseanne and Davey

The term 'elective home education'

The official term for home education in England is elective home education (EHE). Seven of the 11 families were unfamiliar with this term, and most spoke about 'home tutoring' or 'home educating'. Four families in my sample had heard of EHE and offered definitions:

> You get taught at home; you get the same things that you get taught at school, but just at home.
>
> (Vanessa)

> It's you choosing which way you want your child to be educated.
>
> (Jolene)

> They stay at home; they have someone to come in and help them, or you [parent] help them. There are certain books that qualify to the law. Then they [LA] come and check them and say 'That's fine, that's OK'. That keeps you inside the law as well as the children learning what they need to learn.
>
> (Elizabeth)

I understood it to mean that the children do not have to go to school and they can be educated in the way that runs a line between the way I want them to be educated and the way the authority wants them to be educated. So it's within the law.

(Patricia)

These definitions capture the element of choice in home education and how it allows parents greater control over the content and nature of their child's education. Families are aware that EHE meets legal educational requirements.

EHE practices

Research tells us that home educating practices are diverse (Rothermel, 2003). This was reflected within the Romany Gypsy and Showman families interviewed. Just as every family is different, so home education practices varied from family to family. But there was one broad distinction between families: some used a tutor and some educated their children themselves. Seven of the 11 families paid for tuition. Tutors taught children the basics of spelling, reading and writing. Maths and ICT skills were sometimes included, although children were often already competent in using numbers and calculations because of their involvement in the family's business. Most families paid a tutor – not necessarily a qualified teacher – to teach their children in their homes. Two families took their children to a private learning centre on a weekly basis where a qualified teacher tutored them in all curriculum subjects.

Paid tuition, whether by a tutor or in a centre, was generally for one or two hours a week and the children completed homework tasks set by the tutors. The amount of homework depended on the tutor and on the age and ability of the child.

At the time of interview one family was searching for a tutor. According to several mothers tutors were found through word of mouth in the community, but not everyone would share information about their tutors. Families wanted qualified tutors but got no outside help, as local EHE guidance placed the responsibility for funding tutors solely with parents:

Parents may choose to employ other people, such as private tutors, to educate their child, though they themselves will continue to be responsible for the education provided. They will be responsible for ensuring that those whom they engage are suitable persons to have access to children. Parents will therefore wish to satisfy themselves by taking up appropriate references or undertaking Criminal Records Bureau (CRB) checks.

(Saltfield LA, 2010)[1]

Families were vulnerable because tutors of EHE children do not require formal professional qualifications; families simply had to believe their tutors were honest, capable and would provide a suitable education:

It's a good job she [tutor] knows what she is doing because otherwise I would be in a pickle to be honest with you.

(Tina)

If I never had trust in the teacher [tutor] to put me on the right road ... I don't know ... I am not a teacher ... I don't know truly where I would be without the teacher.

(Anona)

Among the four families who delivered home education provision themselves, some bought educational books for a specific Key Stage level in English, Maths or Science. Several families had a planned education routine; others varied what they did from day to day. Patricia kept a diary of activities for Derek, the LA's EHE adviser, to monitor when he visited. Other families used laptops or completed a set number of pages in educational books every week and kept this work as evidence of progress.

Jolene based her children's learning on their interests. For example, they went on a bike ride and then each child wrote up an account of the trip on their laptop. Anita, who is from a Showman family, based her children's learning on the places they travelled through and together they compiled scrapbooks of their routes and visits to historical places of interest. Both these mothers emphasized the importance of getting into a learning routine. Comparing their EHE practices reveals the similarities in educational provision across different Traveller cultures. Perceptions of education were also similar:

Main factors of education, from my point of view ... I think reading, writing, adding up ... things like that is an essential; the top three things. If you have got those, obviously if you can read, then you can learn more. If you can't read you are sort of stuck. If you add up and do sums and timetables ... if you can do things like that so that is good. If you can spell it is a bonus. They are the three most important things. I think socializing, learning to talk to people, learning to do things ... that is good too.

(Patricia)

For me, it's the boys had to be able to read and write. It's learning things ... especially that they have got an interest in. Going to different places and seeing the place. It's much nicer if you are doing history when you are actually at a castle and then you can see it and it sticks in your head better. For me it was better being able to show them the places and tell them history and geography side of it. It made it more exciting.

(Anita)

The families ensured that their children were taught the basics by their parents or tutors. In addition to the academic subjects, the families provided a range of learning activities based on the family's needs, such as cooking, needlework (for girls), caring for horses and dogs and helping out with business activities. Thus EHE often mirrored a vocational, although gendered, apprentice-type model of education. Parents drew on extra input and support from friends and relatives who between them had a range of knowledge and skills to support the education of their children.

Although most families said they did not have specific difficulties with home education, some were worried when they first began educating their children at home. Most relied on neighbours, families or friends who already home educated to advise or show them what to do. Some parents had little confidence about delivering home education, particularly during the early stages:

I felt a bit lost ... I did not know if I was teaching them the right things. I don't want to do wrong by my kids' education.

(Jolene)

Traveller mum Patricia had completed the paperwork for EHE and sent it to the LA in September, but was not visited and registered by the LA until March. She said that a shorter start-up time would have benefitted her family. All the mothers wished to do the best by their children, but some expressed concern about having to wait for annual visits, as they did not know if their provision was adequate. Carol-Anne was reluctant to send her daughter Roseanne to secondary school because her older brother had been bullied there, but at the same time she did not feel confident about taking up EHE so asked the primary school if Roseanne could repeat her final year. Her request was refused. Roseanne told me that:

> She [mum] did not know what she had to do to home educate, she thought if she could keep me in [school] another year, it would just be easier all round.
>
> (Roseanne)

This story illustrates again the fact that Gypsy and other Traveller parents do not reject mainstream school but are left with little choice by their experiences of racism and bullying. EHE can be their only option.

All families had a clear understanding that EHE was their sole responsibility:

> You take them out, you sort them out.
>
> (Anona)

> You have made the choice: you do it.
>
> (Jolene)

Every family appreciated receiving monitoring visits and the follow-up reports. Getting good reports made the parents very proud:

> Visits are every 12 months. They go through all her work. I had the loveliest letter from the education people I ever wished. It was beautiful; it made my year.
>
> (Anona)

Although many felt that EHE was acceptable and suited them, others felt that systems were too lax, allowing some families to use EHE as a smokescreen. Concerns about EHE systems, then, are not limited to government officials. Members of the Romany Gypsy and Showmen communities voiced concerns that the vagueness of the system allows children to slip through the net of education:

> You make the decision, you do it, but I think there a lot of chances that kids can slip through. It's the ideal option for people who don't really want to take their kids to school – EHE – but not for the right reasons. They use it as an excuse and because there is not a lot of back-up I think kids will fail and that's a shame because I do think kids need their education.
>
> (Jolene)

The fact that home-educated children may not receive a suitable education is also an equality issue, and this is reflected in the literature. Traveller education teachers who responded to Ivatts' study (2006; see Chapter 5) suggested that EHE could be used to avoid attendance in school. Because of the extremely liberal EHE system, they said, children lose out, as they do not have equal educational opportunities.

Economic and cultural capital appears to be another equality issue. Bourdieu (1986) defines cultural capital as the forms of knowledge, skills, education and advantages a person has that determine their status in society. Parents who have acquired cultural capital can support their children by giving them the knowledge (dispositions) and resources to succeed. Parents who have less cultural capital are, through no fault of their own, less able to support their children to succeed. Home-educated children are entirely reliant on their families' resources for their education. Consequently, families' financial and cultural capital has a significant impact on the level and standard of educational support and the breadth of learning opportunities in EHE. This was obvious among the families interviewed. Moreover, the low-income families struggled with the financial responsibility of home education and having to fund tutor fees, books and computer equipment.

In summary, observing Romany Gypsies' and Showmen's experiences of EHE revealed the variations among the families and their practices. But there are also similarities, such as the mixing of academic provision with practical learning opportunities. There was evidence of inequalities associated with poverty, ethnicity, race, gender, culture and class, often all experienced simultaneously. Several families wanted their children to have more hours with a tutor but could not afford it. When there was no man living in the house, families felt that mothers would have to rely on uncles or friends to teach their boys a trade or specific practical skills:

> Some Traveller women are on their own and haven't got a husband, they ain't got nobody. My husband taught my children his trade from when they were small. I can understand people what have not got a partner and they are left with three boys of 14, 15 and 16 … what are they going to do if nobody helps them out? So they want to send them to school because they could learn something else.
>
> (Teresa)

The way these inequalities intersected demonstrates the complexity of the lived practices of EHE. The English EHE system has been named as the most liberal of any country in Europe (Badman, 2009). Although a liberal

EHE system may suit many families in England, attention should be paid to the consequent inequalities of the system and their impact upon minority groups' experiences of education.

The next chapter develops an in-depth and appreciative understanding of EHE as experienced by certain Traveller families. Three family stories are documented. Vignettes like those documented here provide graphic, narrative accounts that serve the same purpose in CRT as storytelling and counter-stories do, offering insight into Traveller families' individual experiences of EHE, which are diverse and complex. The vignettes help us towards an informed understanding of Travellers' educational wishes and needs.

Note
[1] The local authority name 'Saltfield' is a pseudonym; EHE guidance notes are available from many local authorities.

Chapter 9

The stories Gypsies, Travellers and Showmen tell

Following customary Critical Race Theory practice, this chapter presents three vignettes to document the authentic voices of Travellers and thus illuminate issues of inequality. *The text in italics and in the discussion section at the end of each vignette are my own words and reflections. All other text in this section is a record of the Travellers' own words.*

Kelly's story

Kelly is 13 years old and an only child. She lives with her mother Anona, a young widow, and her extended family on a small, rural Traveller site. Kelly's experience of mainstream education was very short-lived. Her experience of school and the reasons she was home educated are explained below by her mother.

I started Kelly late at school because we had a bad tragedy – she was something to cling to, perhaps I should not have done that. I was selfish but … I am her mum and she is my only one … I started her at 7. She went in the October. I stayed with her for the first few days, then I got a phone call to say she didn't feel well, so I went to get her … nothing wrong with her. Then the next day same phone call and the teacher never picked up on it, never said a word, never asked 'What is the problem?' Kelly was 7 and they put her in reception; she only did two full weeks until Christmas from October!

I said to my mum 'She's worrying me; she can't keep saying she got this and that'. So my mum talked to her and she said 'I don't like school'. It wasn't that she did not like school, it was the teacher. Because Kelly knew she was going to get told off about something stupid. She never came back with something that she would not do in school – it was never about the work. There were other children in there who would be climbing the walls! I used to think what are they doing? She was never like that, but it was always that she did not have the right plimsolls, fruit, drink … it was always a pick to me … well that was how it felt. So I do think if she got a different teacher or a different school that things would have been very different. They never gave me that option.

I went one day to pick her up … she did have a full day, that day, at school! Kelly said 'I got pulled out today'. 'Oh, what for?' Because she's not a naughty girl … and she said 'This lady pulled me out to give me extra help'. 'Why is she giving you extra help?' You know … surely the teacher should have spoken to me about that, before she just took it on board and done it? Then when I questioned that to the teacher she said 'Well, she's a Traveller, she needs extra help'. Why? She didn't. They just thought Travellers needed that. I didn't like that.

Anona was very unhappy with this school's assumptions about Kelly's needs and the way she was singled out. She was concerned about inequality and Kelly's welfare in school.

I ain't making her unhappy, and that's what I done it [EHE] for. But I do think if the teacher had helped her a bit more, never pulled her out or made her feel different then … Obviously when she went to school she was different because she was the Traveller, which is not nice. I've been there, it's not nice. Secondly, the teacher made her feel different by pulling her out. That's how I feel. They should have asked me before they done it. She's only a child. So that's why I pulled her out. I signed her off the register and done it myself.

I do think school is better and I do truly believe today that if I had sent Kelly to a different school, which I have regretted, not once but a million times … she would have got a different teacher. She would still be in school. A proper education is to understand them. Learn her, she's there to be learnt, not pick on her for what fruit she is eating. I am her mum, I want the best for her. I try, touch wood, to do the best with her.

On reflection Anona said she regretted electing for home education as she has found it financially and educationally difficult, especially because Kelly is dyslexic. Her Mum describes her personal experience of electing for home education and reflects upon the way this process made her feel that Kelly's education and welfare was not of interest to mainstream teachers and professionals.

They [the school] kept phoning: 'Kelly's not in school'. I said 'She's not coming back to that school'. People visited and asked 'Why is she not going back?' So I explained 'She's going to be home tutored'. The lady said 'You've got to sign a letter'. She did it for me and I signed …They never said: 'Well why?' They never said: 'Well can't we try her … we'll put her in a different class or school'. It was just another Traveller out the school. That's how I felt, so I might as well be honest. 'Oh well, we ain't got to mess with her now, that's another one out the way.' That's my feeling. Why bother with her when we can bother with our own. I'm not against nobody, but that is how I felt. I thought, well they are not going to give her the opportunity.

Kelly and Anona are content with the way EHE is working now, but they would like more specialized EHE input. Anona describes their EHE practice below.

We go to, well, I call it a school. You go into a very big room and there are tables and laptops and Kelly does her work on that and she gets homework to bring home with her. I sit every week and do it with her. I thought it was the best thing. She's [the tutor] got equipment, she's got the research, she's a proper teacher.

Kelly likes it there, so it's good you know … at home you are just at home. Kelly gets up on a Thursday and knows she got to go to school, the computer is there. I think it gives them a bit of a space, I think it is good. We've done well … been there for four years.[1] We like it, but they have just turned it into a learning centre now, so we go there, but it's the same thing, same person. We go for two hours on a Thursday. Kelly's got homework then from Thursday to Wednesday, what she does every night at home. We've done tapes, booklets … everything there is in school we have done at home. She'll [her tutor] mark it while Kelly is on the computer and then we start a new week. That's it, that's how it goes, it's good, I think it's very good.

She's got today. She knows that today she has got an hour to set aside for homework. Whether at 9 a.m. or 6 p.m., she'll do it, whenever … but there is an hour set for homework. We have worked really hard but Kelly is dyslexic so that is a bridge now we got to get over together. I am not a teacher but there is nothing we have not got over … sometimes on the Thursday we have had to go back and say 'I don't understand it' [homework set] … She'll [the tutor] explain it … and to be honest when I read it, it does not make no sense to me because I left school when I was 11 myself. So what I do is I write it how I understand it and then I learn Kelly how I understand it … but she could have been getting a better education in school if the teachers had given her that. She could have been learning me … but it ain't gone like that.

EHE is very hard, very hard …The government won't help you with them, not one bit, not half, not anything. You took them out, you got to sort them out. We have to pay and you can't afford to pay twice a week, so I do think they should help us a bit more, because they do it if she's at school.

It seems that Anona's reasons for EHE were twofold: first, her dissatisfaction with the way her daughter was treated differently and, second, her daughter's ensuing unhappiness at school. EHE was a pragmatic choice and this family was making the best of the situation they were in, a finding reflected in Winstanley's (2009) research concerning gifted and talented children. Nevertheless, Anona wished that Kelly had been given more opportunities at school and that they could afford more EHE tuition. Interestingly Anona's response mirrors that of Traveller families in Bhopal and Myers's research, who suggested that lack of support in EHE and school was read as 'the perpetuation of school provision that fails to address Travellers' needs' (Bhopal and Myers, 2009a: 4).

Libby's story

Libby is 15 years old and part of a Showman family. At the time of interview he had just started home education. His family are highly mobile and are 'home' on their winter ground for only about three months of the year, between late November and February. Libby has an older brother who completed mainstream secondary education via distance learning. His mother, Anita, explains a little about their lifestyle and their experiences and views of education.

I am not from a Traveller background, only their father. When I first met him, I still had a house and the way things progressed, we had the boys … but it was so difficult. He could be at Cornwall or Cumbria and I'd have to travel on the Friday to see him and I was just worn out at the end of the weekends so … we actually rented the house out first of all and bought a Showman wagon to see how we would get on. I loved it. When you are knee-deep in mud it's not so good but I loved travelling all over the place. I found it easier … we weren't all so tired and with all the travelling about all together. When we first decided I'd be out full-time, we said we've got to see how it goes. I wanted the boys to have an education, to be able to read and write – the basics.

Eventually we got a piece of land down here and Libby went to primary. They were fabulous, we met the Traveller Team teacher and she was brilliant and organized. When we are travelling we got in a routine, no matter what the weather or how close to the beach we were, we got the work done. Most of the time it was really good … the only hiccup was when Libby went up to secondary school.

Anita had real concerns about her son's welfare at secondary school. Below, she describes the level of unhappiness and stress that attending the school caused him. She also describes her disappointment about their secondary school. Anita compares this experience to the experience at primary, where the school had been well organized, creative and caring. At primary school Libby's travelling experiences were shared with the class to extend their understanding of his lifestyle and different geographical places, which ensured he was not forgotten by his class when he was away.

He did not like the [secondary] school. I think it was because it was so big after being in a little primary. They didn't seem to bother so much with him. There was no interest in him, none of the kids knew who he was when he was back, he got himself all wound up about it. Every time we left, I felt like I was pestering them for work. They would call us up for meetings, which was fine and we'd sit there 'What do you want to learn?' 'Yes we'll sort this out and send work back'. But when we sent work back nobody ever emailed back to say: 'Oh that is good' or: 'You need to work harder on this'. Just … nothing … and Libby hated it. He hated going … he says not, but I don't know if he was being bullied. I don't know. Libby is diabetic and every day it was torturous. The Traveller teacher would meet me at the gate and prise him off me and take him in, but then by 11–11:30 a.m. I would have to go back up there because he got himself so worked up his blood sugars had all gone to pot. It was a nightmare … a nightmare.

It was a shame because he loved the primary school. He loved the teachers. I think because they all took the time with him and kept him involved with the other children so they did not forget who he was. The best thing was a map of England, we'd send postcards and they would stick them on the map and chart where he was. They did bits in class on where we were and it was nice, they all remembered him.

Primary was OK, but going up here [secondary school] I thought AGGHH … I could just picture how he felt going in because they didn't put him in classes where he knew anyone. It must be awful, it's almost like they lose their identity because there are so many. They all knew him at the little school but he was just a number up there … it was not the same. So this time, when we got back I thought, I am not sending him back up there. I just could not face it and he did really, really not want to go … so I said: 'We will sort something out'. Because he will end up ill. It's a shame … but saying that, he's got lots of friends. He's always out with friends. He learns other things you know … His Dad is teaching him soldering. He's out there doing spray-painting this morning!

Libby had travelled across the world with his family and was talented and confident. During the winter when I visited, he had renovated a horsebox singlehandedly and helped build a veranda around their mobile home. He had developed many skills and could build a motorbike from scratch, and he always helped set up and perform their show when they were on the road. Whether this apprentice model of home education offers a suitable education depends on one's understanding of 'suitable'. Below, Anita describes how she and her husband supported their sons' education while they were travelling and details her views on the purpose of education.

Whichever place we went to, we would try and take them out somewhere for the day. I would, from my school days, tell them about places, history and whatever I knew and they would write that up in a scrapbook. I sat there and helped him do it. I've got a little computer. It was interesting. He was sat there at the little table writing it all up. I'd say 'Well here's an interesting bit' … and I thought that was more useful for Libby in his travelling side. His older brother stayed until the end of secondary school but he did not do his exams. He's been to night school and done welding and got certificates and stuff. With this lifestyle that's more useful to them.

Libby can read and write. He's good at maths because he builds a lot with his dad. His dad is always at him about doing the measuring and that, he's good. He can do plumbing, electrics. It sounds awful, but when his friends come down from the village, his conversations seem much more grown up. He can talk about more than they can. Then I think, maybe it's not such a bad thing doing the travelling and seeing other things as well, it broadens your outlook. It's a shame you can't see him [do a show]. He's quite a shy boy really … but when he does the show inside he'll quite happily go on the microphone, there could be 200 people there. Introducing acts and then he'll go up the front because everyone will want to talk to him. He will just sit and talk … it is totally different. But if I say to him 'Just pop up to the shop and get me a paper', he asks me to go with him. He can run circles round other boys. Although they probably know more about dates in history, for everyday living Libby knows a lot more, he's seen a lot more. A lot of things they learn at school, they don't use again after school. The stuff Libby learns he is using every day.

Anita's reasons for home education were Libby's health, identity and his exclusion at secondary school. She was committed to education but suggested that the secondary school curriculum was not necessarily relevant for her sons' careers.

The fact that Libby was highly mobile caused problems at secondary school, whereas his primary school had made distance learning work effectively for him. The primary school enabled this family to feel included even when they were not physically present. Although Showmen do not belong to an ethnic minority culture they are still marginalized by cultural assumptions and, as in this case, by secondary schools' inflexibility and unwillingness to meet the specific learning needs of highly mobile pupils. Libby's story makes the case that EHE was his only available educational option.

Marsha's story

Marsha is 12 years old. She attended nursery and primary school and started home education instead of going to secondary school. Marsha has two younger siblings who are both still at primary school. Her family have their own business and both her father and mother work in their shop during the week. Her mother, Patricia, describes the reasons they decide to home educate Marsha and how the EHE process worked for her.

It was not that I was personally worried about school, because from my experience I would have been worried about nursery school because I did not have none of that. So it wasn't the school that was frightening, nothing like that, it was because she was not happy in going. Marsha was not happy going to the secondary school we picked for her to go to. It got so that she started crying every time it was mentioned. She was unhappy in [primary] school because of the thought of going to the secondary school. It was not just *that* school, it would have been any school. If she'd been different and happy to go there it would not have been: 'Well, you are not going because we are Travellers and you are not going'. She would have gone, but it was just she was not happy so ... it was just the way it worked out, we had the opportunity to do home tutoring, so we done it!

I asked questions because I did not know anything about it [EHE]. I was completely in the dark about it. I just generally asked questions and tried to learn. The only thing that did hold it up for a bit was the headteacher at the secondary school, as he needed to send some papers back. I call them release papers but I don't think that's the word for them. You know, to say that she wasn't going to go no more and she would be home educated.

The inspector was really, really helpful. I did not know anything about it ... I didn't even know if there was a set time to do it, one hour a day or two hours? He said it is 'down to you' and providing everything is done within the 12 months that is fine, they are happy with it. We keep a diary of what she is doing. A lot of things come under it [EHE] that I did not think about ... home economics ... She does a lot of these things so ... He was really good.

What I would say is that we don't have a set week. She does a lot at home that comes under home economics, which is good because she loves cooking so we do that ... She helps me in the shop, normally on a

Wednesday. We haven't got a set time on it like Monday we do this, Tuesday we do this … Wednesday we go swimming. It is sort of random but it all gets fitted in. Some weeks probably we don't do things we have done other weeks, but then we'll do it twice the next week.

For Patricia there were many advantages to EHE. She describes them below and declares her commitment to her daughter's education.

I thought in the beginning I would find a lot of it [EHE] difficult but no, not really. I said, when she said she wasn't going to secondary school: 'Whichever way this turns out, she not going to school so this has got to work'. Once we got down and thought this is the way it has got to be and also they told us a lot of things so it was not hard, it was ok.

Flexible; that is the nice thing. This sounds horrible, but you are not tied to a school, even though the other two [her siblings] go. Her going to school as well would not have come into that, but it is just easier. Because with our culture we are happy with the way she is reaching out and the way she is being teached. You know, some of the things probably she would have been teached now [if she had stayed in school], we would not have been happy about [like sex education]. So she would not have been doing it anyway. I feel like I have got more control.

Patricia's views about primary school were very positive. Below she explains how satisfied she was with her daughter's educational provision and progress at primary school and how this played a part in their decision to choose EHE. She also describes what she sees as the purpose of education.

The [primary] school is wonderful. They have done the groundwork and have given her the basics. She is a wonderful reader, she is a wonderful writer. She is good in lots of things. Probably I would have been different if she was not good at these things. If she was a lower grade or something … I would not have been as eager to try this [EHE]. Whereas she's got the ground basics.

You only get one life; if they can do things … Marsha's been going to her granny's and her aunt's. I know that is making her thrive; she is seeing different things, she is with her family, that is all part of learning anyway and they are happy in doing it. If they are happy they will learn and if they are not happy they will not learn, they will lose interest in school and then it's an ever-decreasing circle isn't it.

Patricia's view of education is holistic; the reason for Marsha's non-transfer to secondary school was to protect her happiness and well-being. Patricia is satisfied with EHE because she has control over the content of Marsha's education and she likes the flexibility. EHE means her daughter can learn and help in their trade; she can socialize with different people and see more of her family.

Discussion

Ladson-Billings (2009) advocates the use of CRT in education and the recognition that storytelling is a way of communicating the experiences and realities of the oppressed. My vignettes tell the stories of Traveller families and highlight how different each family's experience of EHE can be. Analysing these vignettes illuminates a number of equality issues. Kelly experienced discrimination on account of her ethnicity as a Traveller. Libby's secondary school experience was in stark contrast to his primary school experience. The marked lack of interest in and commitment to his emotional, social and learning needs shown by the secondary school reveals the hidden subtleties of 'cultural racism', whereby Showman pupils' social and educational needs are not met due to their being perceived as *different*. Patricia's story confirms that schools are slow to follow up on Traveller children's withdrawal. All three stories make it clear that Traveller children are simply not a school priority.

These accounts also show how the quality of EHE provision depends on the family's resources. Anona struggles with the financial burden of providing appropriate education, particularly as Kelly is dyslexic and Anona admits her own poor literacy skills. Patricia felt able to ask lots of questions to ensure she got EHE right, but had to wait for six months before the LA registered Marsha. It appears that Marsha's home education was very gender-specific. Equality issues concerning EHE thus arise because arrangements are poorly supported and monitored (Cemlyn *et al.*, 2009). The next chapter continues to explore Gypsies' and Travellers' EHE experiences, this time documenting the views of EHE professionals on the challenges caused by current EHE systems and their concerns about the families who feel compelled to home educate.

Note
[1] Before this the family had a tutor who came to the home.

Chapter 10

How Saltfield manages and monitors EHE

The Education Act 1944 set out a parent's right to educate their child at home; this was confirmed in the Education Act 1996. However, the parent is not required to inform the LA or any other public body that they are educating the child at home. LAs therefore encounter serious barriers in carrying out their statutory duty 'to establish the identities, as far as it is possible to do so, of children in the area who are not receiving a suitable education' (DCSF, 2007: 5). The lack of definition in legislation or guidance about what constitutes a 'suitable education' presents authorities with a further barrier to fulfilling their duties (Ofsted, 2010: 1).

This chapter presents a snapshot of Saltfield's EHE systems to demonstrate how EHE works in practice. The names of the three people directly involved in managing, monitoring and administering EHE are pseudonymized. The County Attendance Manager, 'Sheila', holds responsibility for EHE as a small part of her overall role. 'Jane', a part-time administrator, deals mainly with the registration of EHE children and organizes visits to their families by 'Derek', who monitors provision.

Table 10.1: Pseudonyms and roles of professionals

Professional role	Pseudonym
EHE admin support	Jane
EHE manager	Sheila
EHE adviser	Derek

EHE processes and practices vary across LAs in England. Sheila explains the system in Saltfield:

> When we hear of a child who wants to be home educated, or the parents of a child who want to be home educated, we will request that they register on our system, which means sending us back an information form of the details of the child and the education they intend to provide. If they agree then usually after

a while we will do a visit as well, to have a look at provision. If they don't agree or if they don't give us any details or we hear about them but they do not contact us, we will make an effort to contact them. If they still refuse we will do a bit of investigating to see if there are any causes for concern, if there aren't then there is nothing we can do.

(Sheila)

The EHE information form is the first stage of registration. It contains questions about where the child was last educated, if they have an SEN or learning difficulty and whether parents or carers have made an official request for their name to be removed from the school roll. This is because parents of children who leave school must put in a written request to inform their school they are home educating, so that the child is removed from the school roll and can be registered as EHE. The form includes enquiries about the nature of planned home education provision. Questions are asked about learning resources, plans for library use, sports and educational provision and opportunities for contact with other children.

When families return the completed form, Jane, the administrator, arranges for Derek, the adviser, to visit them. Derek's job is to approve and monitor families' home education arrangements; he judges whether a suitable education is being provided. Jane tries to arrange for Derek to visit a family within one month of the receipt of the information form. Reportedly, some families ask to have a little longer to familiarize themselves with EHE, because they want to decide and standardize what they do and wish to have something to show the adviser when he first visits. Other families want the adviser to visit promptly because they want advice. Jane felt that this LA is responsive to different families' needs as they try to comply with such requests.

Once families have registered and provision is approved, progress is monitored annually. Although this may sound a rather formal process, I was told by Jane and by the families too that visits are welcomed because they offer support, advice and feedback. Maintaining positive relationships with families was considered important in facilitating Saltfield's monitoring and support of EHE. As Jane said, 'We can help them to make their education appropriate and they often like that, that reassurance that they are doing OK'.

Judging a suitable education
Ofsted (2010) and Badman (2009) both suggest that the lack of definition in legislation or guidance about what constitutes 'a suitable education'

creates a barrier for local authorities in fulfilling their duties. Saltfield EHE department informs home-educating parents that their children should receive an effective education appropriate to their individual needs and aspirations, and that they should have access to appropriate resources and opportunities to interact with other children and adults. Although EHE does not have to be delivered as a set of discrete subjects, children would be expected to develop knowledge and skills in the three core areas of English, mathematics and science (Saltfield LA, 2011).

The EHE manager, Sheila, told me that judgements regarding the suitability of EHE in Saltfield were based upon the child's reading ability, writing ability and general educational progress. There was an expectation that children should be relatively close to the academic levels of school-aged peers, unless they had particular learning needs that would, in school, have been termed SEN. Monitoring visits played a key part in assessing suitable education provision, as Derek expected to see examples of work so he could observe the child's progress. Where he saw no evidence of adequate educational provision he would suggest specific targets to the parents and if there was still no improvement the family would be ordered to return their child to school. The Education Act 1996 states:

> If a parent ... fails to satisfy the local education authority ... that the child is receiving suitable education, the authority shall serve on the parent ... a school attendance order ... requiring him to cause the child to become a registered pupil at a school named in the order.
>
> (Education Act 1996, section 437)

In Saltfield, School Attendance Orders (SAO) were also served to those families who were known to be providing home education but did not respond to written requests from the LA to provide information about their educational provision. Where parents failed to return children to a named school, court appearances and fines could follow.

Sheila and Jane felt that the assessment process for judging a suitable education was fair and that they considered cultural needs. Jane told me:

> Derek does a lot of visits to Traveller families, for example, and is very aware of their culture and difference and quite happy that this is reflected in the type of education, as long as the sort of basics are included. Derek is seeing that they deal with the basics of literacy and numeracy. If we can achieve annual visits, the adviser notes progress and does advise families on how to

store work done so they can map progression ... so when he goes back on visits he can see. So he knows that they have been doing work and are progressing, although not to a level they would have done if they had stayed in school.

(Jane)

Saltfield LA clearly judges EHE against school standards. McIntyre-Bhatty (2007), however, suggests that doing so is problematic.

Badman's review of EHE in England

The process of generating the Labour Government's review of EHE, and the response to that review (Badman, 2009) , was discussed in Chapter 3. Sheila had provided an LA response as part of the review; indeed, she and Jane had had high hopes for the outcomes of Badman's report and recommendations, but said that local home-educating families had not shared their views. Jane observed that certain home educators made sure their voices were heard but that this happened possibly at the expense of other home educators' needs:

Opposition was mostly from the more capable home-educating parents who thought it would be an interference with their lifestyles. I do not think they had taken enough consideration of children who are not high achievers and whose parents had chosen home education for other reasons.

(Sheila)

The current, unchanged guidance remained the basis for the managers' and administrators' policies and procedures. Still, Sheila did not feel the EHE system was robust:

As far as it goes it is fine but doesn't go far ... There is no means of us knowing the families we don't know, our powers ... we can only intervene if we have cause to ... so ... if that family has not raised its head above the parapet we have no reason to intervene, so I think there are huge safeguarding issues and welfare in the sense of – with some families, we have no idea if they are getting any education or not.

(Sheila)

Even though no changes were made to EHE guidance nationally, this small EHE team had reviewed their own EHE procedures. They had shortened the time between visits from two years to one and updated the information they provide to parents. In addition, they now ask parents to explain the reasons they have chosen to home educate on the information form. Jane confirmed the suggestion in the literature that LAs find the monitoring of EHE challenging:

> It's difficult to work without the backing of something under the law because the area is so wishy-washy. Parents are more aware of their rights, what we can do and what powers we have. We are constrained by what we can do and what the parents want us to do, but we also have to balance that against a child's welfare and safeguarding issues – it is very difficult at times.
>
> (Jane)

There were concerns about the system's ability to ensure that home-educated children receive a suitable education: Jane was frustrated about inadequate staff resources for EHE. She struggled to keep up with the rising number of EHE families coming through the system and said that the whole EHE area was understaffed and under-resourced:

> I am probably missing the odd child here and there ... I flag things up and task them but the sheer volume, I feel like I am drowning.
>
> (Jane)

Although LAs are required to intervene if it appears that home education provision is deemed unsuitable, limited resources, weak guidance and restricted LA duties caused serious ethical and practical challenges for Saltfield's EHE team.

Reasons for EHE

Jane reported that the numbers of home-educated children were rising quickly:

> Quite a few of the ones that come out of school are because they are dissatisfied with school or education being provided or circumstances of the child – like if they are being bullied, or not doing very well. They are not always negative reasons ... quite a few do it for positive reasons.
>
> (Jane)

Interviews with Jane and Sheila confirmed that the grouping of reasons for EHE into positive and negative categories, as seen in the literature (DCSF, 2007; Badman, 2009; Webb, 2010), is evident also in practice. Jane classified the groups who choose EHE for negative reasons into five areas: children with additional learning needs (SEN); Gypsy and Traveller children; children whose parents want to protect them from the increasingly demanding world; gifted and talented children; and, finally, school refusers. These are discussed in turn.

Jane spoke of a significant rise in the number of children with SEN in the LA and those who were under special provision at school, for example for dyslexia. Her view was that as these children's parents became more knowledgeable about SEN they also became increasingly dissatisfied with school provision.

Jane suggested that Gypsy and Traveller children take up EHE 'because of their lifestyle. They don't agree with secondary education or [favour] very limited secondary education'. She said that, although the numbers of non-Traveller home-educated primary and secondary-aged children were nearly equal, the overall numbers of EHE children might include a higher preponderance in the secondary age group because of Traveller choices:

> The [LA] figures might be slightly tipped towards the secondary age because of the Traveller situation. They will educate at primary level and then withdraw immediately at transition time to secondary ... or within a year or two.
>
> (Jane)

Research undertaken by Ivatts (2006) showed that, nationally, twice as many secondary-aged as primary-aged Traveller pupils are home educated.

Jane also referred to the increasing numbers of parents who are, as she put it, 'being very cosseting of their children because the outside world is demanding'. Yet the families she described sounded more like parents who want to protect their children from harming experiences at school and from the distinct lack of appropriate responses by the schools:

> In situations like bullying, parents are very concerned about their child's welfare in school, they show dissatisfaction with the way schools are handling bullying situations ... I often get families saying that their children are still expected to go into school but the school are not doing anything about the bullies, they are not removing them from school, the children still have to go in and face them and they can't have their child crying their eyes out every morning.
>
> (Jane)

She said that a few children had even tried to commit suicide: 'There have been two or three cases where children have got to that point and are now being home educated'.

Bullying is a major reason for home educating (DCSF, 2007). Considering the picture of EHE in Britain as a whole, Gabb (2004) stated that, in 2002, 20 children in all – not Traveller children – committed suicide because of bullying and other pressures in school. Jane, similarly, was not referring directly to Traveller families in her statement, but the concerns she described about bullying, and about the perception of secondary school as a microcosm of a dangerous wider society, echo the views of the Romany Gypsy and Showmen families I spoke to. Interestingly, Badman's (2009) review of EHE in England was triggered by concerns about the safety and suitability of EHE provision. These concerns, coupled with evidence from my discussions with families, certainly suggest that children's safety and educational provision in school is a concern that deserves serious consideration and attention because it is a key factor that prompts families to take up EHE. In reality, school can be a dangerous space for many Gypsy, Traveller and otherwise Othered children. Jane confirmed that many parents are compelled to home educate to provide a safe space for their child:

> People are sometimes just backed into a corner ... they don't know what else to do; often they are making the decision to EHE without the skills to deal with it ... or the resources.
>
> (Jane)

Although my research is focused upon the exclusion of Gypsy and other Travellers, it is clear that more inclusive systems and attitudes would benefit all children.

Jane named gifted and talented children as another group who were frequently home educated due to the failings of the mainstream system: 'The state system does not allow them to fly'. She called the choices of home-educating parents of gifted and talented children a sacrifice:

> I think it is a sacrifice on their part because they have to put so much into home education ... you can see the amount of effort parents put in ... it is astounding! ... Often they do not just have one child but may have three or four – so hats off to them ... they really do well. Exceptionally well in some cases.
>
> (Jane)

Finally, Jane talked about the parents who choose to home educate to avoid prosecution for not sending their children to school. Note that here too she did not suggest these families were Gypsies or Travellers. The parents she spoke about often had numerous issues to deal with in their lives and could not always deal with getting their children to school. It tended to be these families that the LA needed to pursue for registration purposes, as they failed to respond to requests to provide information about their EHE provision and did not agree to monitoring visits.

Obviously Jane's classifications of the types of children who take up EHE are her own, but she is dealing with EHE families on the ground every day. Although I would not claim that her account accurately portrays the situation in Saltfield, her voice is undeniably useful in demonstrating an official perception of the EHE population. Jane's story confirms the key messages in the literature, which suggest that the population of EHE families is diverse, yet also has many commonalities.

Sheila's and Jane's responses also confirm that school (particularly at secondary level) represents a microcosm of wider society and causes many parents to worry about their child's safety and welfare. Consequently, a general pattern is emerging of parents who default to home education provision rather than choosing it for positive reasons, and this is troubling. This issue casts doubts on the way mainstream education treats children who are labelled as different.

Traveller families' use of EHE in Saltfield

The Saltfield LA monitors numbers of EHE children on an annual basis. Between September 2010 and March 2011, 289 children had passed through the EHE system. This means that 289 children were either registered as EHE or waiting to be registered (parents had completed an information form but not been visited). Just over a quarter of these (64) described themselves as Travellers but the data collected did not distinguish among particular Traveller groupings.

Of the total 289 children, slightly over one in ten (30 children) was deemed to have special educational needs; this included six in the cohort of Traveller children (9.4 per cent of the Traveller total). This local data correlates with the proportions recorded in the EHE literature (Badman, 2009; Arora, 2006), and suggests that Travellers make up a significant component of the overall home educating community. The high proportion of children with SEN in the EHE total is also significant. The statistics reveal that 10.4 per cent of home-educated children have some form of additional learning need, and that the same proportion of Traveller children who are home educated have SEN. We thus see how inequality issues can intersect and reinforce barriers to educational inclusion and progression. Schools and educational practitioners need to be reminded of the concept of intersectionality; discrimination should be understood as a matrix of intersecting inequalities.

Speaking about Gypsies and other Travellers' high uptake of EHE at secondary school level, Sheila said: 'They are not getting what they want from school, they don't want to send their children at secondary level, but how do you overcome that, is there an alternative?' She suggested that more needed to be known about the difficulties Travellers experience in secondary school, and saw this as the responsibility of the Traveller Education Service (TES). Treating all Traveller education issues as the sole responsibility of the TES is a limiting script, but in my professional experience I found schools used it frequently. This attitude reflects the adaption of a deficit model of thinking, whereby Gypsies and other Travellers are homogenized as the Other; their needs are assumed to be someone else's responsibility because of their cultural difference. My literature review confirmed that even though the problems Traveller children face in schools are well documented, the government response has remained inadequate and I argue that the prevailing deficit model of thinking explains why.

Neither Jane nor Sheila identified mobility as a reason for Traveller families in Saltfield choosing EHE, although it was widely cited in the literature as the main reason Travellers chose EHE. These professionals' voices thus provide evidence or counter-stories that challenge the dominant discourse on EHE. Jane's and Sheila's stories confirm that it is the problems encountered in secondary school that are key, and not mobility. I am not suggesting that mobility is not a factor for some families, only that dominant discourses that suggest all Travellers take up EHE on account of their cultural itinerancy is inaccurate. Such discourses act to justify obfuscating and disregarding the real reasons Gypsy and Traveller families withdraw their children from school.

The fact that Travellers make up a quarter of all EHE registered children in Saltfield should raise questions about equality in the authority's schools. Jane expressed her concern about equality of opportunity in EHE:

> As an LA employee ... it is their [Travellers'] choice of lifestyle and we are doing the best we can, given the resources we have to support them. As a mother I feel ... I wonder if children are being given opportunity to make a choice ... of whether they want to continue to carry on that lifestyle or develop a different lifestyle. It is not a question that we are wanting to change them, but to give them the opportunity to develop.
>
> (Jane)

Jane's words encapsulate the way in which Gypsy and Travellers are placed in a lose-lose situation. Mainstream school is a place of inequality, but so is

EHE. Although EHE provides what can be called a safe space, it does not facilitate the kinds of opportunities that schools can.

In summary, Jane's and Sheila's stories confirm that EHE families are diverse yet share similarities. They also, though, reveal a worrying trend, which drives parents, and particularly Gypsies and other Travellers, to choose EHE because their children's needs are not being met in school. Jane and Sheila confirm that problems in secondary school drive Gypsies and other Travellers to home educate. Their accounts provide a counter-story that challenges the dominant discourse in which mobility and avoidance of prosecution are the main reasons for Gypsies and other Travellers to opt for EHE. In the next chapter, we return to Travellers' own accounts.

Chapter 11

Choosing EHE

> Crystal went to secondary school. She was offered drugs in the playground. I told the school but they did nothing about it. So I took her out. Alfie was going to go to secondary school. But in the school holidays some boys started picking on him. They would not leave him alone. They told him he would be bullied at school. He would not go. I had one at home anyway so best to keep him home too.
>
> (Vicky)

Most of the Romany Gypsy and Showman families I interviewed felt compelled to take up home education because of problems in school, particularly at secondary level. Seven families spoke about overt bullying by school staff or students. Some talked about the more subtle influences of cultural Othering: their child was picked on and treated differently because they were a Gypsy or Traveller. Many families were concerned about their children's safety and well-being in an environment dominated by a different culture. All the following statements are concerned with secondary schools, except the last:

> Marsha was not happy to go to the secondary school we picked for her to go. Not just that school, any school, it got so that she was crying every time it was mentioned.
>
> (Patricia)

> Ronnie was being bullied and the school locked him in a room by himself. Davey got anxiety at secondary school and that is why he has been pulled out.
>
> (Tina)

> I was being bullied at school and I was unhappy at school, I did not like it. I did not have any friends at this school.
>
> (Courtney)

They did not seem to bother much with him. He hated it, he hated going … he says not but I don't know if he was being bullied.

(Anita)

Well, there was a couple of reasons really … for one main reason I did not like the things what was said in the playground [at primary school], it wasn't things I like my kids to be involved in. The things my kids were having said to them were disgusting … Amos told me about it. Home education is the way to go with Amos anyway, because he's … well he is at home and he was uncomfortable at school.

(Jolene)

Romany Gypsy and Showmen families gave various complex, multi-faceted reasons for home educating their children. One factor was special educational needs. Amos was diagnosed with autism after his mother reported her concerns about his behaviour to their doctor. At least three other children who were currently home educated had been identified as having some form of SEN, and this played a part in the families' decisions to home educate:

Safer to keep her at home, and she wasn't … I would not have said this to her … up to scratch to go to big school, I don't think she would have coped with it.

(Elizabeth)

That's another thing, we've known for 12 months that she is dyslexic but would they have picked that up in school? I don't think they would have done. Because it would have been: 'Oh, she's a Traveller'. That's how I feel about it.

(Anona)

We see that Elizabeth does not feel that her daughter will cope in secondary school and that Anona believes that her child's ethnicity and culture have a negative effect on the school's response to her special educational needs. The Travellers' voices reveal a combination of intersecting inequalities, which indicate that the children's treatment at school depends on whether or not they fit the norm.

Two issues dominated:

- problems with bullying and discrimination in school;
- EHE being seen as affording children a more suitable environment than school.

When Bhopal and Myers (2009a) investigated why Traveller families took up EHE, they also found that the reasons given included negative issues about school and positive aspects of EHE. Both explanations pointed to a range of issues of inequality.

Problems in schools: Bullying and discrimination

Because the reasons for EHE uptake among Traveller families were complex, I wanted to make sure they were correctly documented. After summarizing the problems that the families identified with schools, I checked back with them; they agreed that the list below covers the main problems, particularly at secondary school:

- bullying;
- discrimination (by teachers and children);
- traveller children not being safe;
- being seen/treated differently by teachers;
- traveller children learning things that are not in keeping with their culture.

Bullying

It is common for Traveller children to encounter discrimination, name-calling and racist bullying in school (Lloyd and Stead, 2001). Racism and the assumption of profound cultural difference mean that all Traveller pupils, including those who are not from ethnic minorities, are racialized and viewed as deficient (DePouw, 2012). Seven of my respondents spoke of incidents of overt bullying, and at least four families spoke of wider discrimination and their child being segregated due to being a Traveller. In addition, some children were segregated because of their low literacy levels. If we examine the issues of racism and bullying separately from those of illiteracy and bullying, we can observe the intersection of inequalities encountered by Romany Gypsies and Showman pupils in schools.

RACISM AND BULLYING

Carol-Anne had been bullied in school as a child, and when the same thing began happening to her son she withdrew him. This also affected her younger daughter's education:

My son went to secondary school and had a terrible experience, yes ... because he's a Traveller. He got picked on, even by the teachers. I was not prepared for Roseanne to go through that. We had the same when we went to school, my brother and sisters, so ...

(Carol-Anne)

Courtney, a young Traveller, said she had been bullied for some time at school before she was home educated:

I was being bullied and honestly don't think it was a very good school altogether, I told near enough every teacher in school [about the bullying] but they never said anything about it really, they just said if it happens again come back. I kept going back and back [to teachers for support] but nothing ...

(Courtney)

Her older sister, Vanessa, added:

They should take bullying seriously ... other children have killed themselves. They should not take it lightly ... She [Courtney] is a strong person, she'd come home and have a cry and get on with it ... some children are not like that.

(Vanessa)

Ureche and Franks (2007) completed a study on the views and identities of 201 Roma, Gypsy and Traveller young people in England. They found that 63 per cent of the Traveller children in their study had experienced bullying and physical attacks and 86 per cent had been verbally abused. They confirmed that some of those children were withdrawn because of the bullying they experienced in school. Teresa spoke for many of the Gypsy and Traveller parents I interviewed when she said 'That is a big worry with Traveller children ... bullying – he had a bit of bullying and would not entertain it'.

Cemlyn *et al.* (2009) note that 'racist bullying and harassment of Traveller pupils is the most prominent theme in the literature, combined with inadequacy of many schools' responses' (Cemlyn *et al.*, 2009: 97). Lloyd and Stead's (2001) research confirms that teachers frequently do not believe Travellers' complaints about bullying or simply dismiss them. Courtney and Vanessa's comments confirm this. Tina also remarked on the way teachers do not acknowledge bullying: 'It's the bullying as well; they [school] say it does not happen but it do happen'. Rocky, who came from a

Showman family, was made to stay in the school office so he would not be bullied while he waited for the school bus. His mother discovered this by chance when she picked him up from school one day.

Although seven families cited bullying as a primary reason for choosing home education, others did not mention it overtly – as illustrated in Teresa's initial explanation for home educating her son:

> Usually when Traveller children turn 11 and change schools, they don't usually go to secondary school. It is very rare that Traveller children go to secondary school. I decided to home educate because that way he would still be learning things without having to go through the system of going to school.
>
> (Teresa)

It was only later in the interview, when I asked Teresa what she thought about the positive aspects of EHE, that the issue of bullying surfaced:

> Travellers usually find it hard to mix in secondary school; with EHE there is not a problem with bullying and things like that ... That [bullying] is a big worry with secondary school and Traveller children. I mean he did go to the college [secondary school], but he had a bit of trouble. He had a bit of bullying. He would not entertain that. It's different when you get lots of Traveller children going but when you only have one or two ... when there is a lot [of Traveller children] it is usually OK. Primary was easy because there was about 50 Traveller children ... so they are used to them and they go from when they are small ... then they change [schools]. You usually get other children going from other schools to the college [secondary school] what perhaps have not even had any contact with Traveller children.
>
> (Teresa)

Teresa's words are important for two reasons. First, they afford insight into the perceived difference between primary and secondary schools and the factors that are seen to determine bullying and discrimination. Second, Teresa's initial response about why she home educates is, in my professional experience, a typical response or script, the implication that that is just the way it is – Traveller children don't go to secondary school.

Derrington and Kendall's research (2004) showed that Traveller families saw non-transfer to secondary school as a form of cultural protection of their children. Scripts are stories we might use to protect ourselves. They are powerful historical and ideological foundations that act as a 'system of circular relations which unite structures and practices' (Bourdieu and Passeron, 1977: 203). When Teresa says that Travellers don't go to secondary school, she is using a script – one she may have used when people came and asked why her child was not attending school. The script can defend and protect her decision and her family. However, when I asked more questions, it emerged that her son did attend secondary school for a short period, but that he was bullied and therefore withdrawn. This demonstrates that scripts should not be accepted without question. Critical questions must be asked so that the real reasons come to light. Gypsies' and Travellers' scripts may not initially reveal the racism that members of these communities experience. But my research findings strongly indicate that Gypsy and Traveller families use EHE as a legal way to protect their children from racism in schools.

Scripts relate to habitus, which Bourdieu (1986) describes as the internalized social norms or tendencies that guide a person's behaviour and thinking and drive their actions unconsciously. Racism is driven by these unconscious attitudes, particularly the hidden, subtle forms that perpetuate educational inequality for Travellers.

ILLITERACY AND BULLYING

One Showman family and one Romany/Gypsy family in my sample told me that their children had been bullied because they could not read or write. Marie (a Showman mother) describes how, 'The class were all looking at a certain page in their books, the teacher said "not you, you look at a picture book instead as you can't read or write"'.

Marie asked the school if they could focus more on her son, Rocky's, reading and writing, but was told that this was not possible, as the National Curriculum did not allow it. I was not able to verify this account, as the teacher in question was not named. Nor was it the purpose of my research, which was to listen to Gypsies' and Travellers' voices so as to articulate their reality. Marie's account raises serious equality issues; reading and writing are central to the taught curriculum and have to be supported. Another (Romany/Gypsy) mother's comment suggests Rocky's situation may not be an isolated example:

> My older son went through primary and then up to big school and he could not read or write and they just called him stupid. Secondary school is awkward isn't it … when they get up there … it's a different step up there and I suppose they can't take it.
>
> (Marie)

Education policy has placed much emphasis on embedding basic literacy skills at primary level. Children are undoubtedly disadvantaged if they arrive at secondary school unable to read or write. Romany Gypsies' and Showmen's comments highlight how entering secondary school with low literacy levels can present insurmountable barriers for pupils' inclusion and attainment. These Traveller children were discriminated against on account of their culture, ethnicity and low literacy skills, and this discouraged them from staying on in school.

Discrimination

Discrimination can be defined as the unjust treatment of different categories of people, which leads to oppression (Thompson, 2001). Six families referred to general discrimination and the way in which their children were treated differently as Gypsies or Travellers:

> I don't like this new one [headteacher], she pretends, we can tell. You can walk in a room and know if a person likes you. We have lived this lifestyle for a lot of years. I am 40 and I can tell in a minute and thought … you are playing a game. You have to play the game. You can tell by certain things, tell by her attitude … I can't say he was ever bullied … but I know he felt different. He knowed he was different and he knew the teachers knew he was different and I think they were a little bit more peppi-handed with him.
>
> (Elizabeth)

> I don't think it was more the children, it was more the teachers than children, not violent bullying but they call you square peg compared to other children.
>
> (Shannon)

> It's like we go swimming every Monday. There is a lady there who is swimming instructor, for people who can't swim and every week she tries her hardest. 'Please come in pool.' You can really see she's really wants you to do it – with a school teacher, you want to feel they do want my child to be there – they do want them. But I never got that … Once I had signed that letter to say I pulled her out, I will home educate on my own, never heard from them from that day to this. So it proved to me that they did not

want her there, that is how it seems and I think I was right and I don't regret pulling her out ... not at all ... no, definitely not.

(Anona)

Marie, who came from a Showman family, told me that not one of her seven children was ever invited to the homes of their school peers to play or go to a party, and how this made her feel excluded from the community. She herself had experienced segregation when she was a child:

When I went back everyone said don't play with her, she don't stay around long, and I stood in the corner and felt alone ... then I ended up playing with 'backwards' children ... which suited me and suited them.

(Marie)

The problems of segregation and being constructed as the Other were common to all the families, not just those who were recognized as being from an ethnic minority. Race and racism are apparent but so is the intersection of race with other forms of subordination (Solorzano and Yosso, 2002). It is clear that all Travellers, whatever their ethnicity, experience racism and discrimination. Marie comes from a Showman family whereas Anona is a Romany/Gypsy, yet they feel equally discriminated against on account of their ethnicity and culture. Both women felt that their children were discriminated against in school on account of their learning needs (dyslexia and illiteracy). I present their stories as evidence of inequality in school, which discourages Traveller families from allowing their children to access mainstream education.

It is significant that only two families out of 11 had been asked by the school why they withdrew their children from school. When we talked about this, it was clear that families did want to be asked to explain their reasons:

I decided to take my kids out of school and there was no feedback whatsoever, nobody said 'Is there a problem? Would you like to discuss it?' I just said the boys are not coming back anymore and it was 'OK thank you just send a letter in' ... that was it. If I was a teacher I would like to say: 'Would you like to make an appointment and we'll see if there is any reason or discuss if this is the best move for the children. Do you know what you are getting yourself into? Do you know what they need?'

(Jolene)

> There should be more feedback from school, even though you have made the decision and you can't say they are responsible now ... it's not that ... it is just that ... just like that ... let them go.
>
> (Vicky)

> I think it depends on the problem ... because if it's a high rate [big problem] they will close down on you; they will back the teacher the whole way because they have to ... if its low rate they may help you but then again they see you in a different category. They know it's not going to go any further so they think ... OK we will try and stop it, but if we don't they will pull them out anyway ... and that's how they see it and 90 per cent of Travellers will do that – just pull them out 'coz what's the sense in being tortured.
>
> (Elizabeth)

Kiddle (1999), Derrington and Kendall (2004) and Wilkin *et al.* (2009) have all noted that schools do not always follow up Traveller pupils' absences quickly. My respondents' accounts confirm that not being asked by the school why they are withdrawing their children makes them feel even more isolated and unwanted. Elizabeth suggested schools were reluctant to prioritize Travellers' issues because they assumed that their children would be withdrawn at some point anyway.

Faced with these conditions, many Traveller parents simply give up on school. All the Traveller children who were being home educated at the time of interview had previously attended school. Eight families had withdrawn their children at the point of transition to secondary school or during secondary school. Most parents had limited experience of school education themselves and only two had experienced secondary school. Many were particularly anxious about secondary school and their children's safety and well-being there. They had little confidence about being able to challenge inequality issues in school.

The language used in education to discuss cultural difference is an issue of power. It is not the Travellers in this field who control 'what can be said and thought, but also who can speak, when, where and with what authority' (Hall, 1992: 290). We have heard from Travellers that they want to discuss issues around their children's education in school, with the staff there. The recommendations they make are sensible, but they point to the negative comments and assumptions made by schools about mobility and the Othering of the children. It is seen as almost inevitable that Traveller children will at some point be withdrawn from school, thus perpetuating inequality of opportunity.

Safety in school

> Traveller people are not looking on school and her learning to read and write and sit in uniform, we are not worried about that – what we are worried about is what is going on in that school.
>
> (Elizabeth)

Anxieties about school spaces were often centred on the behaviour and language of non-Traveller pupils. We heard that Crystal was offered drugs in the playground and that Jolene's children reported other children using language in the school playground that hers were not allowed to use. Jolene felt that the playground was a space where her children would learn to swear. Sixteen-year-old Roseanne thought back to her transition to secondary school and reflected on how her ethnicity as a Traveller affected her security, self-confidence and learning:

> Going into school mixing with new people and then being a Traveller as well feels like a big weight on your shoulders. Like the whole world is on your shoulders. If you go into school confident and happy you sit there and take it in, if you are nervous you worry about things, what will happen at playtime instead of thinking about what you should be – your school work.
>
> (Roseanne)

Safety was also about strength in numbers. The fact that so few Traveller pupils transfer to secondary school means that those who do are socially isolated in an environment where they feel vulnerable. Bhopal and Myers (2009a) observed how Traveller parents refer to secondary school life as unsafe, whereas they perceive their own culture as a safe place.

O'Connor (2007) observes how being faced with unfamiliar places can evoke feelings of anticipation, curiosity and excitement or feelings of fear, anxiety and bewilderment. She asserts that negative feelings will be reduced if we have a sense of being eagerly awaited or know we will be treated with respect. Sadly for the Traveller children who did transfer, they were not supported or respected and the assumptions that teachers held about them obstructed their progress and discouraged them from staying on.

Treatment by teachers

> I think if they paid as much attention to Traveller children as other children then I don't think there would be so much of a problem … but where you have a Traveller child and another child in a fight, then the Traveller child is always to blame. When you are in school you can always see Traveller children falling behind. I don't think they pay Traveller kids as much attention as they should pay them.
>
> (Tina)

Remember Tina's earlier remark at the beginning of Chapter 6? She said that if the school had been better, she would not have needed to home educate her children. Caprice felt the same; she comes from a Showman family and was herself a gifted and talented pupil. Now in her twenties, she reflected on her school experiences:

> I liked the little school; I was a 'gifted and talented' pupil and top of the class with everyone at primary. I liked the little school … they [primary school] used to send out work packs for when travelling and I did them because I wanted to. The [primary] school wasn't racist. I dropped down at secondary. I hated it … I felt excluded. At secondary school you were just a number, not a pupil.
>
> (Caprice)

Caprice had wanted to complete her secondary education, but said that school staff did not bother with her because they assumed that she would follow a career in the family business and did not need a school education. Yet Caprice *had* wanted to complete her education, because it offered an alternative vocational pathway should she have wanted to move away from the Showman lifestyle. Her story highlights the use of scripts concerning cultural difference and the effects of intersecting inequalities. Caprice's educational needs as a gifted and talented student were seemingly undermined by the school's cultural assumptions about her background. Stereotypical assumptions had been made about her vocational trajectory and learning needs; they prevented educational progression and led to her withdrawal from school. Interestingly, Ofsted reported back in 1999 that teacher expectations of Gypsy Traveller children were unreasonably low, and named raising teacher expectations as a priority. My own research and the literature indicate that little has changed: teachers still make stereotypical assumptions about Gypsy, Roma and Traveller students' abilities and aspirations.

Traveller children's exclusion from secondary school is perpetuated in part by Traveller parents' scripts that they 'don't do school', and teachers' scripts which assume that such children don't want school and will at some stage be withdrawn anyway. These scripts exclude Travellers from the classroom. We must therefore ask critical questions about Travellers' withdrawal from school. Although EHE professionals in Saltfield documented the families' reasons for taking up EHE, what would be done with these responses was not clear. The data could certainly provide important evidence of the issues in school. Discussions between EHE staff, schools and families are crucial in order to challenge the damaging way the prevailing scripts perpetuate discourses of exclusion. As Bourdieu and Passeron (1977) suggest, habitus is not fixed or permanent, and can be changed.

The problems these children encountered in school can be described as push factors. They push Gypsy and other Traveller children out of school and into EHE. But there is a second major reason for families taking up EHE.

EHE: A suitable education?

The suitability of education was a central topic of discussion in my interviews with EHE professionals and Travellers alike. Professionals spoke about how a suitable education was to be judged and Travellers referred to the positive benefits of EHE. These benefits can be described as the pull factors that attract families to take up EHE. The stories told so far have considered the push factors that motivate EHE uptake, suggesting that families use EHE as a means to protect Gypsy and other Traveller children from the negative experiences they face in mainstream school. However, all the Traveller families interviewed strongly believed that EHE had real benefits, and named the following:

- Children are safe and protected.
- Children can continue learning but without attending school.
- Parents have better control over the things children learn.
- EHE is flexible and can fit into the family routine.
- More time is spent with family.
- Learning as part of EHE tends to be more suited to Gypsy and Traveller lifestyles and what children are likely to need to get on in later life.
- Children can stick to a way of life they are used to.

The EHE professionals in Saltfield judged EHE to be suitable if it included the basics (English, maths and science), and the families held a similar view. It is fair to suggest that all 11 families agreed that reading and writing comprised a suitable education:

> In school you learn geography, history, art. They are useful for Traveller children but they don't need to know them things for everyday life. It's the basics like ... English and a good knowledge and writing and obviously reading, mathematics is good and computers. I mean he can do all the computer things like that ... It's helpful for them.
>
> (Jolene)

> It's the basics. We don't really need the other ones [subjects in school]. Obviously he is not going to go to university and go get a degree to be a doctor or you know whatever ...
>
> (Elizabeth)

> The basics is to help get him along. They need to get a driving test and they have to learn to read, it's good to learn to read because it's harder now than what it used to be. See all them things plus computers help them with that ... because it's all done on a computer now isn't it?
>
> (Teresa)

> I think they should go to school, but not in secondary school. I don't think they help you enough. They think you are grown up now, they don't need help. I think it is better anyway when you learn one to one. You are concentrating, not distracted by anything.
>
> (Courtney)

> I think they have had a good education. As well as learning all the basics ... they have seen something of the world ... Tony was in Germany when he was 11. Off with German friends ... teaching him a few words. Much more exciting than sat in a classroom. But we talked about it. I'd said if they are not learning, I don't want them struggling, they have to be able to read and write. To get on in life you have to be able to do that. If they wanted to do something different ... they still need that ... you can progress

from there, even if you don't want to do a Fair life … You must
still have the basics.

(Anita)

These responses highlight how Traveller families felt that EHE enabled
their children to continue learning, while keeping them safe and protected
in the community, away from school. Learning was also focused upon the
Traveller lifestyle and what children needed to help them get on in later life.
EHE enables parents to select, organize and transmit the knowledge and
skills they feel are relevant for their children, rather than being subject to
the dominant culture's schooling in which they hold little power or agency.
Readers of these excerpts might say that some Traveller parents do not
seem to have high aspirations for their children, but aspirations depend
on a person's own cultural background and expectations and what is most
important and relevant to family and community needs. As Jolene stated:
'It is not always the education that gets you a job, sometimes it's a bit of
knowledge about everything'.

Families carrying out EHE combined structured reading and writing
opportunities with vocational skills. Children in Gypsy and Traveller
communities are often involved in their family businesses or occupations
from an early age. EHE enables children to spend more time with their
families and be taught occupational skills at the same time – almost a
vocational, apprenticeship model of education. Families wanted to access
qualifications when they were relevant. Libby's brother did not complete
his GSCEs, but did attend a further education college to complete a welding
course so he could build fair rides and fix cars, lorries and motorbikes.
Marsha, whose family owned a shop, studied maths, English and science,
completed work on a computer, helped with the cooking at home and
with accounting and customer service in the business. These tales provide
important counter-stories to those that depict Gypsy and other Traveller
families as uninterested in or unable to provide a suitable education.

The reality of discrimination and prejudice means that Gypsy and
Traveller families seldom have equal opportunities in obtaining mainstream
employment (Cemlyn *et al.*, 2009). Tina explains how, in this context of
inequality, completing school and obtaining qualifications is actually of
little use:

They [education officials] had the cheek to say that Ronnie got to
go to secondary school and to college. My cousin passed all the
exams you know … she can't get a job. As soon as she mentions
she is a Traveller or place she lives at they don't want to know.

> But her friend [non-Traveller] applied with less qualifications and got the job.
>
> (Tina)

None of these families is discounting the importance of education and learning, but they are in some cases discounting the significance of the mainstream curriculum in advancing their children's employment opportunities. These choices might be described as self-exclusionary, but they indicate parallels with those of working-class young people which are informed by 'a realistic appraisal of the objective probability of their succeeding in a stratified education system in which opportunities for social mobility are severely limited' (Gewirtz and Cribb, 2009: 48).

Romany Gypsies' and Showmen's stories illuminate direct experiences of inequality and challenge the negative language and literature that describes Travellers and education. Their stories challenge the dominant discourse that implies Travellers' choice of EHE is driven by their mobility. Not a single family in my sample suggested that mobility was the reason for their taking up EHE. The interviews with the families reveal instead that school systems are failing to provide a safe and inclusive culture and an inclusive and relevant curriculum to children from a range of backgrounds. The children's safety and well-being is of central concern and their families perceive EHE as a safe space:

> Yes, happiness is top priority. If children are not happy they will not learn … you know … and if they are not interested they won't learn … so we try to push them into things they are happy in.
>
> (Patricia)

> Children need to want to learn; they learn as they go along. My children were not happy to go so EHE made it easier.
>
> (Marie)

In the concluding section of this chapter I will return to answer the questions posed in Chapter 1:

- Why do Gypsies and other Traveller families choose home education?
- What are Gypsies and Travellers' experiences and perceptions of home education?
- What equality issues are evident in Gypsy and other Traveller families' use of home education?

EHE as a safe space

Ivatts (2006) suggested that Gypsies and other Traveller families might be compelled to take up EHE because of the discrimination they face in schools. The Traveller families' stories in this book confirm this, while showing that their reasons for EHE are complex, interwoven and centred on various inequalities, influenced by both push factors and pull factors.

Push factors: issues in school

My research has found that Gypsy and other Traveller families are reluctant to keep their children in school, particularly at secondary level, because of the racism, discrimination and bullying they endure there. Moreover they reported that schools failed to respond appropriately to racism and bullying or to children's learning needs. The Travellers' stories documented in my research confirm that families' decisions to home educate are shaped by overt and covert racism in school. Traveller families took up EHE to be rid of problems in school, not because they were uninterested in educating their children. For these families EHE was the only viable educational option. Mainstream school systems were not accessible, inclusive or relevant for many of the Traveller families I spoke to.

The discriminatory dominant discourse, which combines racial stereotyping with assumptions of profound cultural difference, portrays Travellers as a group who are deficient and operates behind a smokescreen about mobility. The expectations of Traveller pupils held by schools remain low and these children are allowed to drop out of school with ease. Their withdrawal does not provoke any concern as it is framed as the Travellers' cultural choice, not their response to racial discrimination. Besides, the withdrawal of Traveller children happens to be in the interest of schools.

Pull factors: the safety offered by EHE

For the Traveller families interviewed, EHE provides an alternative, preferable educational space. EHE enables children to continue learning in compliance with the law but without having to contend with the bullying and discrimination suffered at school. Home-educating Gypsy and Traveller parents have greater control over the content of their children's education, so learning can be tailored to specific knowledge and skills that children need to get on in later life. Children spend more time with their families and are taught a variety of skills at first hand. EHE is a safe space.

The notion of safe spaces is not new, and has been explored previously in research about education (Toynton, 2006; Blackwell, 2010; Rollock, 2012). The concept of a safe space or positive space originated in the women's movement, and the first safe spaces identified were gay bars and consciousness-raising groups (Kenney, 2001). A safe space represents a physical space or community where marginalized people can express themselves and act without feeling uncomfortable on account of their race, culture, gender or identity. In terms of education, a safe space is one that welcomes, educates and addresses the needs of Others; a place where pupils are not harmed verbally, physically, institutionally or culturally (Kumashiro, 2000).

Myers *et al.* (2010) found that Gypsy and Traveller families attempt to create protective environments for their children; my respondents' accounts confirm these findings. Jolene says: 'Home education they are here, among Travelling people'. Elizabeth described EHE as a protective bubble: 'Girls are sometimes in a bubble situation but that is their lifestyle'. EHE allows Traveller children to be close to their families and removes them from negative and potentially damaging emotional experiences at school:

> Home education is nice ... I don't think they get into too many things ... in all fairness they don't need half the things they learn in school. The good things are that they can stick to the way of life.
>
> (Jolene)

> You are away from the school environment and I think it's good because you can be taught at home. I don't think you learn less or more than in school, it's just better because you are at home.
>
> (Courtney)

> EHE gives you a chance to grow up and turn into what you want instead of being like everyone else. If you are in school and being bullied you think 'Well, to stop being bullied I need to be more like so and so who is not bullied ... I need to be different' ... it affects your confidence. If you are bullied in secondary school it follows you through, it really does. You feel like you won't fit in anywhere. You don't want to get a job because you think it will be like secondary school.
>
> (Roseanne)

However, the fact that EHE is an escape route from persisting inequitable school systems is itself discriminatory. EHE fails to ensure that all the children reliably receive a suitable education at home; monitoring and support systems are weak and children are ultimately dependent on their families' resources. Listening to each Traveller family's stories indicates that all are doing the best they can to educate their children with the resources they have, but some struggle to access the financial and social resources required. In addition, several families were relying on tutors to provide a suitable education, yet there is no guarantee that the tutors do so, and no regulation of the people who families pay to deliver home education. Further, gender trajectories are more pronouncedly divergent in EHE: girls receive different and generally less varied educational experiences than boys do. Excluded from mainstream school, home-educated Gypsy and Traveller children may not be able to develop the kind of critical intelligence about the dominant society that might enable their communities to challenge the racist power structures that exclude them in the long term.

I am not arguing for or against EHE. Rather I seek to illuminate continuing issues of inequality within educational spaces. Since education is both a fundamental right in itself and a means of realizing other rights (Save the Children, 2001), denying Gypsy and Traveller children full educational opportunities in schools disadvantages them still further and restricts their life chances. These issues are summarized in the final chapter.

Chapter 12

Educational spaces and inequality

> How we are seen determines in part how we are treated: how we treat Others is based on how we see them; such seeing comes from representation.
>
> (Dyer, 1993: 1)

Ways of seeing

CRT scholars assert that racism is ever-present and that we should never forget this; Dyer's words encapsulate why Gypsies and Travellers experience such racism and are treated the way they are. The stories told in this book say a great deal about inequality in school and EHE. They highlight certain key issues:

- Covert racism is evident in the mainstream literature, as it generally implies that Travellers opt for EHE for cultural reasons and questions their commitment to the education of their children.

My study, however, showed clearly that:

- Not one family mentioned mobility as a reason for EHE.
- Traveller parents are dedicated to their children's well-being and deeply interested in their education.
- Travellers flee from overt racial injustice in schools and the social system, and EHE is the only legal refuge.

Thus, we see that:

- EHE is not a matter of free choice for Traveller families. It provides an educationally safe space but does not afford equality of educational opportunity.
- EHE provision is dependent on a family's material and social resources.
- EHE isolates Gypsies and Travellers within their own communities and thus maintains their social exclusion.

In reality, EHE precipitates a cycle of disadvantage for the most vulnerable Traveller children and their families. It is clear that ultimately neither school nor EHE provides these children with 'an efficient education suitable to their needs' (Education Act 1996, section 7). As Traveller parent Tina puts it:

> There aren't really any good things [about EHE] other than not having the hassle … If the children had not had the hassle, then they would still be in school. So it isn't really a good thing. If things in school changed there would be no EHE as Travellers would be quite happy to keep the child in school. But then when you get no support from school so you got to pull them out. You still get no support when you pull them out … you are still left. The best thing about EHE is that the child is not being bullied or called 'Pikey'; that is the best thing about EHE. There are lots of downfalls because they don't give you enough support because they say you pulled them out, but it's down to them that you pull them out, it's what's happening in the school but they don't understand that. I don't know …
>
> (Tina)

The families are trapped in a lose–lose situation. Current education systems and spaces allow the needs of the most vulnerable children in society to be neglected. Article 28 of the UNCRC establishes a child's right to education and stresses that this right must be achieved on the basis of equal opportunity (UNICEF, 2005), but this is seldom the case for Gypsy and Traveller children.

Interest convergence: Letting schools off the hook

When a pupil moves to home education the school may well find it convenient, as the child might have been bringing down their attendance and attainment data. The pressure of measured school standards may explain why withdrawal to EHE is rationalized by the system: it absolves the school and LA of failure to meet their statutory Public Service Equality Duty (PSED) and frees them from having to acknowledge the child's problems, let alone examine and confront them.

Derrington and Kendall (2004) suggest that EHE enables LAs and the dominant society to deal with Traveller students' non-attendance, a classic example of the CRT principle of interest convergence. It is convenient to frame EHE as the cultural choice of Travellers, because revealing the real reasons behind their uptake of EHE may expose the systems that socially exclude Travellers. Delgado confirms that dominant groups often justify their power through stories that offer stock explanations and construct reality in ways that maintain their privilege (Delgado, 1989: 24).

Racism is deep-rooted. Culturally racist attitudes, which discriminate on grounds of culture rather than (solely) skin colour, do not typically use the word 'race', but race nonetheless remains an issue (Barker, 1981; Gillborn, 1995). CRT scholars use the notion of interest convergence to illuminate how dominant White interests prevent real advancements in race equality. Equality for minorities will be tolerated only when their successes also serve the broader interests of Whites (Gillborn, 2006, 2008). The failure to reveal information about the reasons why many families resort to EHE, and the failure of institutions to address the underlying problems, exemplify the symbolic and structural systems that prevent advancements in race equality for Traveller communities. Interest convergence inhibits action to tackle racism, social exclusion and inequality.

The nature of oppression

Mainstream literature and language focuses, as I have shown, on Travellers' cultural difference and portrays Travellers as undeserving. Moreover, reports (DfES, 2005; Ureche and Franks, 2007; Bhopal and Myers, 2009a) on Travellers' experiences in education are based on Gypsy, Roma and Traveller groups who are recognized as ethnic minorities. But EHE was a safe space for Showmen and Romany Gypsies too, and I have presented their stories together to emphasize how *all* Traveller groups are subjected to racism and educational inequalities on account of their perceived cultural differences. Experiences of racism and bullying and schools' lack of response to educational needs are evident in the stories Travellers tell us in this book, and are true for Showmen and Romany/Gypsy families who are, in the CRT sense, not White because they are all minority groups. All are seen as Others and excluded on this basis.

Danaher (2001) warns of the dangers of underestimating the detrimental effect of perceived cultural difference in school, lest children fall into unformed spaces in between. EHE represents an unformed space in between school and home into which children are permitted to fall by allowing Traveller parents to withdraw them from school.

A wealth of evidence shows that education is a key determinant of life chances. As well as being a right in itself, education is an enabling right, allowing individuals to develop the skills, capacity and confidence to secure other economic opportunities.

(EHRC, 2010)

Educational provision should be designed to ensure that all children have a realistic opportunity to become autonomous persons and to benefit the communities they live in (Save the Children, 2001; Brighouse, 2007). But this is not the case for Gypsy and Traveller children. My findings show that they are ultimately denied a choice of futures. Yet, as Brighouse (1997) asserts, all adults have an obligation to contribute to the provision of education to every child – it is a matter of justice. All children have the right to respect, but Gypsy and Traveller communities are not respected by the dominant culture.

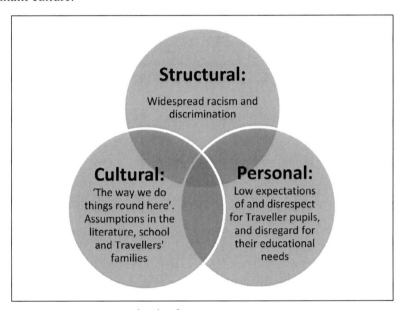

Figure 12.1: Intersecting levels of oppression

Thompson (2001) analyses oppression at three intersecting and interacting levels: personal, cultural and structural. This model helps us to understand the complexity of educational inequality for Traveller communities:

- The feelings, attitudes and actions that characterize teachers' prejudice and shape their practice reflect inequality at the 'personal' level.

- The commonalities and assumed consensus transmitted in the EHE literature reinforces Travellers' 'cultural' differences. Schools' and families' scripts similarly endorse the cultural stereotype that 'Travellers don't do school'.
- At the 'structural' level we find the prevalence of racism and of interlocking patterns of power and oppression (Thompson, 2001).

Thompson's model is the framework for the recommendations that follow for combating the educational inequalities identified in this book.

Oppression and Traveller education

Because equality policies and procedures are in place, some may assume that issues of race and racism have been resolved (Craig *et al.*, 2012: 5). However, the following facts remain:

- Equality legislation has not yet halted racism, and inclusion policies and incentives are often short term.
- Moreover, racial discrimination and inequity has disappeared almost entirely from the political agenda (Gillborn *et al.*, 2012).

What can be done?

To eradicate the prevailing educational inequalities that beset Travellers, the reality of racism must be acknowledged at government level. Combating it must be made a priority within education policy and practice.

If education is right for Traveller children, it will be inclusive and right for all children (Ivatts, 2005). Making it right necessitates a curriculum that is critical, creative and intellectually challenging, and which draws on and values cultural capital across different communities and cultures. Schools need to rethink how they engage with Traveller communities and cultures so that they create educational spaces and a curriculum in which children feel valued and safe. Particular areas require scrutiny:

Training and guidance

- Teachers need to recognize, understand and respect the multiplicity of cultures their pupils represent; doing so requires an in-depth understanding and celebration of the diversity of their pupils' backgrounds.
- Initial and in-service training must include informed and critical discussions of culture, ethnicity, and positive identity formation, led if necessary by outside specialists.

- The complex, embedded relationship between culture, power and inequality must be understood by all those involved in educational provision at statutory level, along with a particular awareness of the inequalities Gypsy and Traveller children experience in schools and of the PSED to dismantle these equalities.
- Informed, high-quality guidance and models of good practice in working with Gypsy, Roma and Traveller pupils should be made easily available and be widely disseminated. The DCSF (2009b) produced useful guidance materials to support schools in raising the achievement of Traveller pupils. Republishing them would be straightforward; all that is needed is the will to do so.

School policy and practice

- Schools must build positive relations with Gypsy and Traveller parents, to improve school access and inclusion and to disrupt the commonly accepted scripts that Gypsies and Travellers are not interested in education.
- Dealing with incidents of racist bullying and victimization swiftly, and communicating to Traveller parents that this is done, is the responsibility of everyone who works with children; if this is done reliably and effectively, trust will be earned.
- If any parent wants to opt for home education, schools must ask for and record their reasons. The discussions arising from this process could resolve the problems in school, meaning the child could stay.
- Schools should listen to Gypsies' and Travellers' ideas about what a suitable education consists of and how each child's needs should be met, and should take account of these ideas in their policies and practice.
- Continuing Professional Development for schools and LAs should include discussion of the views voiced by parents in these communities:

'I think reading, writing, adding up … things like that are essential, they are the top three things.'

'I think it depends on what they want to do when they get older really … it's nice to know about history but it does not really help you in the future does it really … just depends on each person.'

'A good education is learning things especially that you have got an interest in. Going to different places and seeing the places.'

'It's the general seeing life. Businesswise it is something you have got to do and that is another thing they learn. There are some things in life that you have to do, that you don't really like. Dealing with customers you always have to put on a smiley face. It's another part of learning life ... hard going sometimes ... just something you have to do ... be pleasant to some people who are not very nice.'

Teachers and school managers could begin by discussing some of these comments.

Improving EHE

If EHE is still to be offered as a legal educational alternative, it requires much improvement. The first steps would be to:

- Clarify the definition of a suitable education: Badman recommended that it be a broad, balanced, relevant and differentiated curriculum 'that enables home educated children to expand their talents and career prospects' (Badman, 2009: 9);
- Give parents adequate information and guidance about how to ensure that EHE provision is suitable;
- Commission further research on the complex intersections of inequality that affect home-educating families. Additional resources can then be made available to ensure that all children receive a suitable education.

Conclusion

The experiences and perceptions of EHE documented in this book illuminate our understanding of educational spaces. They offer a new angle of vision and a seldom-shared way of viewing the world; they also illuminate some complex issues in education. Educators and scholars who apply critical theoretical thinking recognize that race is a central issue in education but that its consequences are difficult to address. The reality of racism and other compounded inequalities impede Gypsy and Traveller children's access to a suitable education, whether in school or through EHE. Social injustice perpetuated by school and the education system causes EHE numbers to rise. Unequal educational opportunity is currently the lot of Traveller children and of other groups, such as gifted and talented children and children deemed to have SEN, who often resort to EHE. This has to change.

There can be no equality without a fundamental shift in power and thinking (Lawrence, 2012). Travellers' experience of inequalities in school can be eliminated only through a collective educational focus that responds to the documented evidence of Travellers' unequal treatment and comes to respect difference and value diversity as benefitting the educational outcomes of all children. Travellers' voices can inform education policy and practice if there is a collective will to hear their voices. As Weiss (1991) observes:

> It takes an extraordinary concatenation of circumstances for research to influence policy directly … (rather) research helps people consider issues, it helps them think differently, it helps them reconceptualise what the problem is and how prevalent it is, it helps them discard some old assumptions, it punctures old myths.
>
> (Weiss, 1991: 308)

The evidence presented in this book makes a strong case both for the radical transformation of school education to combat racism and for a critical reconsideration of EHE, so that children who use it do receive a suitable home education. Much still needs to be done to ensure that Traveller communities and all those who are Othered are given the opportunity to receive a good education, be it at school or at home.

References

Acton, T. (2004) 'The past, present and future of Traveller education'. Paper presented at a conference on 'Working Together: Raising the educational achievement of Gypsy and Traveller children and young people', University of Greenwich, London.

Apple, M.W. (2000) 'Away with all the teachers: The cultural politics of homeschooling'. In Cooper, B.S. (ed.), *Home Schooling in Full View*. Greenwich: Information Age Publishing, 75–95.

Arora, T. (2002) 'Research report on home education in Kirklees'. Online. http://tinyurl.com/nvgg7r4 (accessed October 2010).

— (2006) 'Elective home education and special educational needs'. *Journal of Research in Special Educational Needs*, 6 (1), 55–66.

Attewill, F. (2013) 'First traveller student at Cambridge University to graduate with a first'. *The Metro* 25 June. Online. http://metro.co.uk/2013/06/25/first-traveller-student-at-cambridge-university-to-graduate-with-a-first-3856436/ (accessed March 2014).

Badman, G. (2009) *Review of Elective Home Education in England: A report to the secretary of state*. London: The Stationery Office.

Barber, M. and Mourshed, M. (2007) 'How the world's best performing schools come out on top'. Online. http://mckinseyonsociety.com/how-the-worlds-best-performing-schools-come-out-on-top/ (accessed October 2011).

Barker, M. (1981) *The New Racism: Conservatives and the ideology of the tribe*. London: Junction Books.

BBC (2004) 'CRE examines treatment of gypsies'. 17 October. Online. http://news.bbc.co.uk/1/hi/England/3751214.stm (accessed November 2010).

BERA (2011) 'Ethical guidelines'. Online. www.bera.ac.uk/publications/ethical-guidelines (accessed August 2013).

Bhopal, K. (2001) 'Gypsy Travellers and education: Changing needs and changing perceptions'. *British Journal of Education*, 52 (1), 17–61.

Bhopal, K. and Myers, M. (2008) *Insiders, Outsiders and Others: Gypsies and identity*. Hatfield: University of Hertfordshire Press.

— (2009a) 'A pilot study to investigate reasons for Elective Home Education for Gypsy and Traveller Children in Hampshire'. Hampshire: Hampshire County Council.

— (2009b) 'Gypsy, Roma and Traveller pupils in schools in the UK: Inclusion and "good practice"'. *International Journal of Inclusive Education*, 13 (3), 299–314.

Blacker, S. (1981) *Case Studies in Home-Education*. MEd thesis, University of Sussex.

'Blackmun, H.' (2006) In Rawson, H., and Miner, M. (eds), *Oxford Dictionary of American Quotations*, 2nd edn. Online. www.oxfordreference.com/view/10.1093/acref/9780195168235.001.0001/q-author-00008-00000161 (requires subscription) (accessed March 2014).

Blackwell, D. (2010) 'Side-lines and separate spaces: Making education anti-racist for students of color'. *Race, Ethnicity and Education*, 13 (4), 473–94.

Blok, H. (2004) 'Performance in home-education: An argument against compulsory schooling in the Netherlands'. *International Review of Education*, 50 (1), 39–52.

Bourdieu, P. (1986) 'The forms of capital'. In Richardson, J. (ed.), *Handbook of Theory and Research for the Sociology of Education*. New York: Greenwood, 241–58.

Bourdieu, P. and Passeron, J.C. (1977) *Reproduction in Education, Society and Culture*. London and Beverley Hills: Sage.

Bowers, J. (2012) 'Gypsies and Travellers: their lifestyle, history and culture'. Online. www.travellerstimes.org.uk/downloads/lifestyle_history_and_ culture_24052010111520.pdf (accessed March 2014).

Brighouse, H. (1997) 'Two philosophical errors concerning school choice'. *Oxford Review of Education*, 23 (4), 503–10.

— (2007) 'Educational justice and socio-economic segregation in schools'. *Journal of Philosophy of Education*, 41 (4), 575–90.

Bruggemann, C. (2012) *Roma Education in Comparative Perspective*. Bratislava: United Nations Development Programme.

Bryman, A. (2008) *Social Research Methods*. Oxford: Oxford University Press.

Burman, E. (1994) 'Interviewing'. In Banister, P., Burman, E., Taylor, M., Tindall, C. and Parker, I. (eds), *Qualitative Methods in Psychology: A research guide*. Buckingham: Open University Press, 49–71.

Carmichael, S. and Hamilton, C.V. (2001) 'Black power: The politics of liberation in America'. Originally 1967. Excerpts reprinted in Cashmore, E. and Jennings, E. (eds), *Racism: Essential readings*. London: Sage.

Carper, J.C., and Tyler, Z.P. (2000) 'From confrontation to accommodation: Homeschooling in South Carolina'. *Peabody Journal of Education*, 75 (1/2), 8–19.

Cemlyn, S., Greenfields, M., Burrett, S., Matthews, Z. and Whitwell, C. (2009) *Inequalities Experienced by Gypsy and Traveller Communities: A review*. Research Report 12, Equality and Human Rights Commission.

Chattoo, S. and Atkin, K. (2012) 'Race, ethnicity and social policy: Theoretical concepts and the limitation of current approaches to welfare'. In Craig, G., Atkin, K., Chattoo, S. and Flynn, R. (eds), *Understanding Race and 'Ethnicity': Theory, history, policy and practice*. Bristol: Polity Press, 19–41.

Children, Schools and Family Select Committee (2010) *The Review of Elective Home Education: Government response to the Committee's second report of session 2009–10*. (HC 2009–10, 423). London: The Stationery Office. Online. http://www.publications.parliament.uk/pa/cm200910/cmselect/ cmchilsch/423/423.pdf (accessed October 2010).

Clark, C. (2006) 'Who are the Gypsies and Travellers of Britain'. In Clark, C. and Greenfields, M. (eds), *Here to Stay: The Gypsies and Travellers of Britain*. Hatfield: University of Hertfordshire Press, 10–27.

Clough, P. and Nutbrown, C. (2007) *A Student's Guide to Methodology*, 2nd edn. London: Sage.

Collins, J., Noble, G., Poynting, S. and Tabar, P. (2000) *Kebabs, Kids, Cops and Crime: Youth, ethnicity and crime*. Annandale, NSW: Plutopress.

Commission for Racial Equality (CRE) (2006) *Common Ground: Equality, good relations and sites for Gypsies and Travellers*. London: CRE.

Commission of the European Communities (1984) *Report from the Commission to the Council on the Implementation of Directive 77/486 on the Education of Children of Migrant Workers* (COM84-54). Brussels: Commission of the European Communities.

Coxhead, J. (2007) *The Last Bastion of Racism: Gypsies, Travellers and policing*. Stoke-on-Trent: Trentham Books.

Craig, G., Atkin, K., Chattoo, S. and Flynn, R. (eds) (2012) *Understanding Race and 'Ethnicity': Theory, history, policy and practice*. Bristol: Polity Press.

Cram, F. (1992) Ethics in Maori Research: Working Paper, Department of Psychology, University of Auckland.

Cresswell, J.W. (2009) *Research Design*, 3rd edn. London: Sage Publications.

Cryer, P. (2011) 'Educational resources for postgraduate research'. Online. http://postgradresources.info/index.htm (accessed October 2011).

D'Arcy, K. (2008) 'How Can Young Travellers' Participation within Education be Promoted?' MA diss., Brunel University.

— (2010) 'Strand B: ELAMP Strand B: The Back on Track Initiative'. Online. www.natt.org.uk/sites/default/files/documents/Final_Strand_B_report.pdf (accessed December 2010).

— (2011) 'Parenting and Early Years support for Traveller communities'. *Runnymede Bulletin*, Issue 367, Autumn 2011.

Danaher, P.A. (1995) 'Show children's perceptions of their schooling experiences'. *Unicorn*, 21 (3), 43–50.

— (2001) 'Travellers under the Southern Cross: Australian show people, national identities and difference'. *Queensland Review*, 8 (1), 77–85.

Davis, K. (2008) 'Intersectionality as buzzword: A sociology of science perspective on what makes a feminist theory successful'. *Feminist Theory*, 9 (1), 67–85.

Delgado, R. (1989) 'Storytelling for oppositionists and others: A plea for narrative'. *Michigan Law Review*, 87 (2), 411–41.

Delgado, R. and Stefancic, J. (2001) *Critical Race Theory: An introduction*. New York: New York University Press.

Department for Children, Schools and Families (DCSF) (2007) *Elective Home Education: Guidelines for Local Authorities*. London: DCSF.

— (2008) 'Identifying Gifted and Talented learners – getting started'. Online. http://preview.tinyurl.com/qd6mj24 (accessed October 2011).

— (2009a) 'Elective Home Education: An overview of evidence'. Online. http://webarchive.nationalarchives.gov.uk/20090810175049/dcsf.gov.uk/foischeme/_documents/dfes_foi_774.pdf (accessed September 2010).

— (2009b) *Moving Forward Together: Raising Gypsy, Roma and Traveller achievement*. The National Strategies, Booklet 1: Introduction. London: DCSF.

— (2010) 'Independent review of Elective Home Education'. Online. http://webarchive.nationalarchives.gov.uk/20100403014058/http://dcsf.gov.uk/everychildmatters/ete/independentreviewofhomeeducation/irhomeeducation/ (accessed September 2010).

Department for Education (DfE) (2011) 'The Education Bill'. Online. www.education.gov.uk/aboutdfe/departmentalinformation/educationbill (accessed August 2011).

— (2013) 'Improving educational outcomes for children of travelling families'. Online. www.education.gov.uk/consultations/downloadableDocs/consultationDocument[1].pdf (accessed March 2014).

Department for Education and Skills (DfES) (2003) *Aiming High: Raising the achievement of Gypsy Traveller pupils.* London: DfES.

— (2004) 'Every Child Matters'. Online. www.education.gov.uk/publications/standard/publicationDetail/Page1/DfES/1081/2004 (accessed October 2010).

— (2005) 'Ethnicity and Education: The evidence on minority ethnic pupils aged 5–16'. Online. www.education.gov.uk/publications/eOrderingDownload/DFES-0208-2006.pdf (accessed September 2010).

Department of Education and Science (DES) (1967) 'Children and their primary schools: The Plowden report'. London: HMSO.

— (1985) 'Education for all: The report of the committee of enquiry into the education of children from ethnic minority groups: the Swann report'. London: HMSO.

DePouw, C. (2012) 'When culture implies deficit: Placing race at the centre of Hmong American education'. *Race Ethnicity and Education*, 15 (2), 223–39.

Derrington, C. (2007) 'Fight, flight and playing white: An examination of coping strategies adopted by Gypsy Traveller adolescents in English secondary schools'. *International Journal of Educational Research*, 46 (6), 357–67.

Derrington, C. and Kendall, S. (2004) *Gypsy Traveller Students in secondary schools.* Stoke-on-Trent, Trentham Books.

— (2008) 'Challenges and barriers to secondary education: The experiences of young Gypsy Traveller students in English secondary schools'. *Social Policy and Society,* 7 (1), 119–29.

Devine, D., Kenny, M. and Macneela, E. (2008) 'Naming the "Other": Children's construction and experiences of racism in Irish primary schools'. *Race, Ethnicity and Education*, 11 (4), 369–85.

Diener, E. and Crandall, R. (1978) *Ethics in Social and Behavioural Research.* Chicago: University of Chicago Press.

Dixson, A.D. and Rousseau, C.K. (2005) 'Are we still not saved: CRT in education ten years later'. *Race, Ethnicity and Education,* 8 (1), 7–27.

— (2006) *Critical Race Theory in Education: All God's children got a song.* London and New York: Routledge.

Doherty, M. (2011) 'Cuts to Traveller Education Services'. Online. www.acert.org.uk/blog/2011/09/24/cuts-to-traveller-education-services/ (accessed November 2011).

Drudy, S. and Lynch, K. (1993) *Schools and Society in Ireland.* Dublin: Gill and Macmillan.

Du Bois, W.E.B. (2002) 'The Negro college'. In Provenzo, E.F. (ed.) *Du Bois on Education.* Walnut Creek, CA: AltaMira Press, 243–52.

Dyer, R. (1993) *The Matter of Images: Essays on representations.* London: Routledge.

Education Act 1996 (c. 56) Online. www.educationengland.org.uk/documents/pdfs/1996-education-act.pdf (accessed 13 May 2014). London: HMSO.

Education Otherwise (2009) 'Downloadable documents relating to the Badman review'. Online. http://www.educationotherwise.net/?option=com_content &view=article&id=130:downloadable-documents&catid=255:the-badman-review&Itemid=220 (accessed February 2011).

Elementary Education Act 1870 (c. 75) Online. www.educationengland.org.uk/ documents/acts/1870-elementary-education-act.html (accessed 13 May 2014). London: HMSO.

Equality and Human Rights Commission (EHRC) (2010) *How Fair is Britain? Equality, human rights and good relations in 2010.* London: EHRC.

Equality and the Roma Education Fund (2011) 'From Segregation to Inclusion: Roma pupils in the United Kingdom – a pilot study'. Online. http://tinyurl.com/ pqx3sll (accessed March 2014).

European Commission (2004) 'The situation of Roma in an enlarged European Union'. Luxembourg: Office for the European Communities Official Publication. Online. http://ec.europa.eu/social/BlobServlet?docId=99&langId=en (accessed February 2011).

— (2011) 'Communication from the Commission to the European Parliament, the Council, the European Economic and Social Committee and the Committee of the Regions: An EU framework for national Roma integration strategies up to 2000'. Brussels: European Commission.

European Dialogue (2009) 'New Roma communities in England: The situation of Roma from new member states of the European Union and the role of Local Authorities in their settlement and inclusion'. Online. http://equality.uk.com/ Resources_files/strategicguide.pdf (accessed March 2014).

Fenton, S. (2003) *Ethnicity*. Cambridge: Polity Press.

Fidyk, A. (2013) 'Scapegoated in schools: Reading a collective Roma narrative'. In Miskovic, M. (ed.), *Roma Education in Europe: Practices, policies and politics.* Oxford: Routledge.

Foster, B. and Norton, P. (2012) 'Educational equality for Gypsy, Roma and Traveller children and young people in the UK'. *The Equal Rights Review,* 8, 85–112.

Frankfort-Nachmais, C. and Nachmais, D. (1992) *Research Methods in the Social Sciences.* London: Edward Arnold.

Fulcher, J. and Scott, J. (2003) *Sociology*, 2nd edn. Oxford: Oxford University Press.

Gabb, S. (2004) 'Home-schooling: A British perspective'. Online. www.seangabb. co.uk/academic/homeschooling.htm (accessed July 2010).

Galloway, D. (2003) 'Special issue on home education'. *Evaluation and Research in Education,* 17 (2/3), 61.

Gewirtz, S., and Cribb, A. (2009) *Understanding Education: A sociological perspective.* Cambridge: Polity Press.

Gillborn, D. (1995) *Racism and Anti-Racism in Real Schools.* Buckingham: Open University Press.

— (2002) *Education and Institutional Racism.* London: Institute of Education, University of London.

— (2005) 'Education policy as an act of white supremacy: Whiteness, Critical Race Theory and education reform'. *Journal of Education Policy,* 20 (4), 485–505.

— (2006) 'Critical Race Theory beyond North America: Toward a transatlantic dialogue on racism and anti-racism in educational theory and praxis'. In Dixson, A.D. and Rousseau, C.K. (eds), *Critical Race Theory in Education: All God's children got a song*. Oxon: Routledge, 243–69.

— (2008) *Racism and Education: Coincidence or conspiracy?* Oxon: Routledge.

— (2010) 'The White working class, racism and respectability: Victims, degenerates and interest-convergence'. *British Journal of Educational Studies*, 58 (1), 2–25.

Gillborn, D. and Youdell, D.C. (2000) *Rationing Education: Policy, practice, reform and equity*. Buckingham: Open University Press.

Gillborn, D., Rollock, N., Vincent, C. and Ball, S. (2012) 'You got a pass, so what more do you want? Race, class and gender intersections in the educational experiences of the Black middle class'. *Race, Ethnicity and Education*, 15 (2), 121–39.

Grant, C.A. and Zwier, E. (2012) 'Intersectionality'. In Banks, J.A. (ed.) *Encyclopedia of Diversity in Education*. Washington: Sage Publications, 1263–71.

Grix, J. (2004) *The Foundations of Research*. Hampshire: Palgrave.

Guba, E.G. and Lincoln, Y.S. (1985) *Naturalistic Inquiry*. London: Sage Publications.

— (2005) 'Paradigmatic controversies, contradictions and emerging confluences'. In Denzin, N.K. and Lincoln, Y.S. (eds) *Sage Handbook of Qualitative Research*. 3rd edn. London: Sage, 105–17.

Hall, S. (1992) 'New ethnicities'. In Donald, J. and Rattanski, D.A. (eds), *Race, Culture and Difference*. London: Sage, 252–9.

Hancock, I. (2002) *We are the Romani People*. Hatfield: University of Hertfordshire Press.

Hopwood, V., O'Neill, L., Castro, G. and Hodgson, B. (2007) 'The prevalence of home education in England: A feasibility study'. Department for Education and Skills. Online. www.parliament.uk/deposits/depositedpapers/2008/DEP2008-1324.pdf (accessed February 2009).

Housee, S. (2012) 'What's the point? Anti-racism and students' voices against Islamophobia'. *Race, Ethnicity and Education*, 15 (1), 101–20.

Hylton, K. (2012) 'Talk the talk, walk the walk: Defining Critical Race Theory in research'. *Race, Ethnicity and Education*, 15 (1), 23–41.

Ivanov, A., Collins, M., Grosu, C., Kling, J., Milcher, S., O'Higgins, N., Slay, B. and Zhelyazkova, A. (2006) *At Risk: Roma and the displaced in Southeast Europe*. Bratislava: UNDP Regional Bureau for Europe and the CIS.

Ivatts, A. (2005) 'Inclusive school – exclusive society: The principles of inclusion'. In Tyler, C. (ed.) *Traveller Education: Accounts of good practice*. Stoke-on-Trent: Trentham Books, 1–10.

— (2006) *Elective Home Education: The situation regarding the current policy, provision and practice in Elective Home Education for Gypsy, Roma and Traveller children*. London: Department for Education and Skills.

Jordan, E. (2001a) 'Interrupted learning: The Traveller paradigm'. *Support for Learning*, 16 (3), 128–34.

— (2001b) 'Exclusion of Travellers in state schools'. *Educational Research*, 43 (2), 117–32.

Juridical Review (1985) 'Mr Justice Woolf in the case of R v. Secretary of State for Education and Science, *ex parte* Talmud Torah Machzikei Hadass School Trust (12 April 1985)'. *The Times*, 12th April 1985.

Kendall, S. and Atkinson, M. (2006) *Some Perspectives on Home Education.* Slough: NFER.

Kenney, M.R. (2001) *Mapping Gay LA: The intersection of place and politics.* Philadelphia, PA: Temple University Press.

Kenrick, D. and Clarke, C. (1999) *Moving On: The Gypsies and Travellers of Britain.* Hatfield: University of Hertfordshire Press.

Kenrick, D. and Puxon, G. (1995) *Gypsies under the Swastika.* Hatfield: University of Hertfordshire Press.

Kershen, A.J. (2011) 'Series editor's preface'. In Law, I. and Swann, S., *Ethnicity and Education in England and Europe: Gangstas, geeks and Gorjas.* Surrey: Ashgate, xiii.

Kiddle, C. (1999) *A Voice for Themselves.* London: Jessica Kingsley.

Knowles, G. (2011) 'Diversity, equality and educational achievement'. In Knowles, G. and Lander, V., *Diversity, Equality and Achievement in Education.* London: Sage, 1–17.

Knowles, G. and Lander, V. (2011) *Diversity, Equality and Achievement in Education.* London: Sage.

Kukova, S. (2011) *Romani Children at Risk in the Child Protection System in Bulgaria.* Sofia: Bulgarian Helsinki Committee.

Kumashiro, K.K. (2000) 'Toward a theory of anti-oppressive education'. *Review of Educational Research*, 70 (25), 25–53.

Kvale, S. and Brinkman, S. (2009) *Interviews: Learning the craft of qualitative research interviewing.* Thousand Oaks: Sage.

Ladson-Billings, G. (2009) 'Just what is CRT and what is it doing in a nice field like education?' In Taylor, E., Gillborn, D. and Ladson-Billings, G. (eds), *Foundations of Critical Race Theory in Education.* London: Routledge, 17–37.

Ladson-Billings, G. and Tate, W.F. (1995) 'Towards a Critical Race Theory of education'. *Teachers' College Record*, 97 (1), 47–68.

— (2006) 'Towards a Critical Race Theory of education'. In Dixson, A.D. and Rousseau, C.K. (eds), *Critical Race Theory in Education: All God's children got a song.* Oxford: Routledge, 11–31.

Lander, V. (2011) 'Coming from a Traveller Background: Gypsy, Roma and Traveller children: living on the margins'. In Knowles, G. and Lander, V., *Diversity, Equality and Achievement in Education.* London: Sage, 97–111.

Law, I. (2011) 'EDUMIGROM research'. Paper presented at a seminar at Roehampton University, Roehampton, March.

Lawrence, P. (2012) '"Race", education and children's policy'. In Craig, G., Atkin, K., Chattoo, S. and Flynn, R. (eds), *Understanding Race and 'Ethnicity': Theory, history, policy and practice.* Bristol: Polity Press, 151–67.

Leicestershire Together (2013) 'Gypsies and Travellers – The truth'. Online. www.leicestershiretogether.org/gypsy_travellers_the_truth.pdf (accessed July 2013).

Leonardo, Z. (2002) 'The souls of White folk: Critical pedagogy, whiteness studies and globalization discourse'. *Race, Ethnicity and Education*, 5 (1), 29–50.

Levinson, M.P. (2007) 'Literacy in English Gypsy communities: Cultural capital manifested as negative assets'. *American Educational Research Journal*, 44 (1), 5–39.

— (2013) 'Integration of Gypsy Roma children in schools'. In Miskovic, M. (ed.), *Roma Education in Europe: Practices, policies and politics*. Oxford: Routledge.

Levinson, M.P. and Sparkes, A.C. (2006) 'Conflicting value systems: Gypsy females and the home–school interface'. *Research Papers in Education*, 21 (1), 79–97.

Liebrow, E. (1993) *Tell Them Who I Am*. New York: Free Press.

Liegeois, J. (1998) *School Provision for Ethnic Minorities: The Gypsy paradigm*. Hatfield: University of Hertfordshire Press.

Litowitz, D.E. (2009) 'Some critical thoughts on Critical Race Theory'. In Taylor, E., Gillborn, D., and Ladson-Billings, G. (eds), *Foundations of Critical Race Theory in Education*. London: Routledge, 291–311.

Lloyd, G. and McClusky, G. (2008) 'Education and Gypsy Travellers: Contradictions and significant silences'. *International Journal of Inclusive Education*, 12 (4), 331–45.

Lloyd, G. and Norris, C. (1998) 'From difference to deviance: The exclusion of Gypsy Roma and Traveller pupils from school'. *International Journal of Inclusive Education*, 2 (4), 359–69.

Lloyd, G. and Stead, J. (2001) '"The boys and girls not calling me names and the teachers to believe me": Name calling and the experiences of Travellers in school'. *Children and Society*, 15, 361–74.

Lloyd, G., Stead, J., Jordan, E. and Norris, C. (1999) 'Teachers and Gypsy Travellers'. *Scottish Educational Review*, 31, 48–65.

Lubienski, C. (2000) 'Whither the common good? A critique of home schooling'. *Peabody Journal of Education*, 75, 95–122.

— (2003) 'A critical view of home education'. *Evaluation and Research in Education*, 17, 167–78.

Macpherson, W. (1999) *The Stephen Lawrence Inquiry: Report on the inquiry by Sir William Macpherson of Cluny*. London: HMSO.

Macura-Milovanovic, S. and Pecek, M. (2013) 'Attitudes of Serbian and Slovenian student teachers towards causes of learning underachievement among Roma pupils'. *International Journal of Inclusive Education*, 17 (6), 629–45.

Marks, K. (2010) 'ELAMP Strand A: Final report and impact study (2009-10)'. Online. www.natt.org.uk/sites/default/files/documents/Final_Strand_A_report. pdf (accessed January 2011).

Marks, K. and Rowlands, M. (2010) *Home Access on the Move: Providing for mobile families – guidance notes for Local Authorities and Schools*. Leeds: National Association of Teachers of Travellers and Other Professionals (NATT+).

Matsuda, M., Crenshaw, K., Delgado, R. and Lawrence, C. (1993) *Words that Wound: CRT, assaultive speech and the first amendment*. Boulder, CO: Westview Press.

May, S. (2012) 'Critical Multiculturalism and Education'. In Banks, J.A. (ed.), *Encyclopedia of Diversity in Education*. 4 vols. Washington: Sage, vol. 3, 473–9.

Mayers, K. and Grosvenor, I. (2001) 'Policy, equality and inequality: From the past to the future'. In Hill, D. and Cole, M. (eds), *Schooling and Equality: Fact, concept and policy*. London: Kogan Page.

McIntyre-Bhatty, K. (2007) 'Interventions and interrogations: An analysis of recent policy imperatives and their rationale in the case of home education'. *Education, Knowledge and Economy*, 1 (3), 241–59.

McKinney, R. (2001) *Different Lessons: Scottish Gypsy/Travellers and the future of education*. Edinburgh: Scottish Traveller Consortium.

Miles, M.B. and Huberman, A.M. (1994) *An Expanded Sourcebook: Qualitative data analysis*, 2nd edn. London: Sage.

Miskovic, M. (ed.) (2013) *Roma Education in Europe: Practices, policies and politics*. Oxford: Routledge.

Monk, D. (2004) 'Problematising home-education: Challenging "parental rights" and "socialism"'. *Legal Studies*, 24 (4), 568–98.

— (2009) 'Regulating home education: Negotiating standards, anomalies and rights'. *Child and Family Law Quarterly*, 21 (2), 155–85.

Morris, R. and Clements, L. (eds) (1999) *Gaining Ground: Law reform for Gypsies and Travellers*. Hatfield: University of Hertfordshire Press.

Murushiakova, E., Popov, V. and Kovacs-Cerovic, T. (2007) *Advancing Education of Roma in Bulgaria: Country assessment and the Roma Education Fund's strategic directions*. Budapest: Roma Education Fund.

Myers, M., McGee, D. and Bhopal, K. (2010) 'At the crossroads: Gypsy and Traveller parents' perceptions of education, protection and social change'. *Race, Ethnicity and Education*, 13 (4), 533–48.

National Fairground Archive (2012) 'From Van Dwellers to Showmen's Guild'. Online. www.nfa.dept.shef.ac.uk/history/worlds_fair/articles/vans.html (accessed May 2012).

Nelson, J. (2011) 'Home education in England: Accessing "hard-to-reach" communities and the politics of research'. Paper presented at the British Educational Research Association Early Career Researcher Conference, Institute of Education, London, September.

Neuman, A. and Aviram, A. (2003) 'Homeschooling as a fundamental change in lifestyle'. *Evaluation and Research in Education*, 17 (2/3), 132–43.

Nutbrown, C. and Hannon, P. (2003) 'Children's perspectives on family literacy: Methodological issues, findings and implications for practice'. *Journal of Early Childhood Literacy*, 3 (2), 115–45.

O'Connor, A. (2007) *The Early Years Foundation Stage: Primary national strategy*. Online. http://www.ndna.org.uk/Resources/NDNA/Generic%20Folders%20 2/10/40.%20EYFS%20supporting%20transitions.pdf (accessed May 2014). London: DCSF.

O'Higgins, N. (2010) 'It's not that I'm a racist, it's that they are Roma'. *International Journal of Manpower*, 31 (2), 163–87.

Ofsted (1999) *Raising the Attainment of Minority Ethnic Pupils – School and LEA responses*. HMI Ref: 170. London: Ofsted.

— (2001) *Managing Support for the Attainment of Pupils from Minority Ethnic Groups*. London: Ofsted.

— (2003) *Provision and Support for Traveller Pupils*. HMI Ref: 455. London: Ofsted..

— (2010) *Local Authorities and Home Education*. London: Ofsted.

Open Society Institute (2007) 'Equal access to quality education for Roma, Vol. 1'. Online. www.opensocietyfoundations.org/sites/default/files/1summary_20070329_0.pdf (accessed October 2013).

Petrie, A. (2001) 'Home-education in Europe and the implementation of changes to the law'. *International Review of Education,* 47 (5), 477–500.

Phoenix, A. (2009) 'De-colonising practices: Negotiating narratives from racialised and gendered experiences of education'. *Race, Ethnicity and Education*, 12 (1), 101–14.

Piper, H. and Garratt, D. (2005) 'Inclusive education? Where are the Gypsies and Travellers?' Paper presented at the British Educational Research Association Conference, Glamorgan, 14–17 September.

Pizarro, M. (1999) 'Adelante! Towards social justice and empowerment in Chicana/o communities and Chicana/o Studies'. In Parker, L., Deyhle, D. and Villenas, S., *Race Is … Race Isn't: Critical Race Theory and qualitative studies in education*. Oxford: Westview, 53–83.

Quarmby, K. (2013) *No Place to Call Home: Inside the real lives of Gypsies and Travellers*. London: One World Publications.

'Racism' (2012) In *Oxford Dictionaries*. Online. www.oxforddictionaries.com/definition/english/racism (accessed March 2014).

Ray, B.D. (2000) 'Home-schooling for individuals' gain and society's common good'. *Peabody Journal of Education*, 75 (1/2), 272–93.

Reich, R. (2002) 'Testing the boundaries of parental authority over education: The case of homeschooling'. In Madeco, S. and Tamir, Y. (eds), *Moral and Political Education*. New York: New York University Press, 275–313.

Reinhartz, S. (1992) *Feminist Methods in Social Research*. Oxford: Oxford University Press.

Reynolds, M., McCartan, D. and Knipe, D. (2003) 'Traveller culture and lifestyle as factors influencing children's integration into mainstream secondary schools in West Belfast'. *International Journal of Inclusive Education*, 7 (4), 403–14.

Roithmayr, D. (1999) 'Introduction to Critical Race Theory in educational research and praxis'. In Parker, L., Deyhle, D. and Villenas, S., *Race Is … Race Isn't: Critical Race Theory and qualitative studies in education*. Oxford: Westview, 1–6.

Rollock, N. (2012) 'The invisibility of race: Intersectional reflections on the liminal space of alterity'. *Race, Ethnicity and Education,* 15 (1), 65–84.

Rothermel, P. (2002) 'Home-education: Aims, practices and outcomes'. Paper presented at the British Educational Research Association Conference. Online. www.leeds.ac.uk/educol/documents/00002197.htm (accessed August, 2010).

— (2003) 'Can we classify motives for home-education?' *Evaluation and Research in Education*, 17 (2), 74–89.

Rousseau, C. and Tate, W. (2003) 'No time like the present: Reflecting on equity on school mathematics'. *Theory into Practice*, 42 (3), 210–16.

Runnymede Trust (1997) 'Islamophobia: A challenge for us all'. Online. www.runnymedetrust.org/uploads/publications/pdfs/islamophobia.pdf (accessed August 2013).

Saltfield Local Authority (LA) (2010) 'Choosing to educate your child at home: Information for parents/carers'.

Kate D'Arcy

Save the Children (2001) *Denied a Future? The right to education of Roma, Gypsies and Traveller children in Europe.* London: Save the Children Fund.

— (2007) *Early Years Outreach Practice: Supporting early years practitioners working with Gypsy, Roma and Traveller families; with transferable ideas for other outreach early years workers.* London: Save the Children Fund.

Shenton, A.K. (2004) 'Strategies for ensuring trustworthiness in qualitative research projects'. *Education for Information*, 22, 63–75.

Showmen's Guild of Great Britain (1987) *All the Fun of the Fair.* Showmen's Guild of Great Britain. Online. www.nfa.dept.shef.ac.uk/index.html (accessed May 2014).

Sikes, P. (2007) 'Methodology, procedures and ethical concerns'. Paper presented at the University of Sheffield Ed.D. weekend, October.

Smith, L.T. (1999) *Decolonizing Methodologies: Research and indigenous peoples.* London and New York: Zed Books.

Smith-Maddox, R. and Solorzano, D. (2002) 'Using Critical Race Theory, Freire problem posing method and case study research to confront race and racism in education'. *Qualitative Inquiry*, 8, 66–84.

Solorzano, D.G. (1997) 'Images and words that wound: CRT, racial stereotyping and teacher education'. *Teacher Education Quarterly*, 24 (5), 5–20.

— (1998) 'CRT, racial and gender micro-aggressions and the experiences of Chicana and Chicano scholars'. *International Journal of Qualitative Studies in Education*, 11, 121–36.

Solorzano, D.G. and Yosso, T.J. (2002) 'Critical Race methodology: Counter-storytelling as an analytical framework for education research'. *Qualitative Inquiry*, 8 (23), 23–44.

Spiegler, T. (2009) 'Why state sanctions fail to deter home education: An analysis of home education in Germany and its implications for home education policies'. *Theory and Research in Education*, 7 (3), 297–309.

Staunaes, D. (2003) 'Where have all the subjects gone? Bringing together the concepts of intersectionality and subjectification'. *Nova*, 2, 101–11.

Stobart, G. (2008) *Testing Times: The issues and abuses of assessment.* London: Routledge.

Stonewall (2003) 'Profiles of Prejudice'. Online. www.stonewall.org.uk/documents/profiles.doc (accessed July 2013).

Stovall, D. (2006) 'Where the rubber hits the road: CRT goes to high school'. In Dixson, A.D. and Rousseau, C.K. (eds), *Critical Race Theory in Education: All God's children got a song.* Oxford: Routledge, 233–43.

Takiki, R. (1993) *A Different Mirror.* Boston, MA: Little, Brown.

Tate, W.F. (1997) 'Critical Race Theory and education: History, theory and implications'. *Review of Research in Education*, 22, 195–247.

Taylor, E., Gilborn, D. and Ladson-Billings, G. (eds) (2009) *Foundations of Critical Race Theory in Education.* Oxford: Routledge.

Taylor, L.A. and Petrie, A.J. (2000) 'Home-education regulations in Europe and recent UK research'. *Peabody Journal of Education*, 75 (1/2), 49–70.

Te Awekotuku, N. (1991) *He Tikanga Whakaaro: Research ethics in the Maori community.* Wellington: Manatu Maori.

Teranishi, R.T. (2002) 'Asian Pacific American and Critical Race Theory: An examination of school racial climate'. *Equity and Excellence*, 35 (2), 144–54.

Thomas, G. (2009) *How to do your Research Project*. London: Sage.

Thompson, N. (2001) *Anti-Discriminatory Practice*, 3rd edn. London: Palgrave.

— (2011) *Promoting Equality*, 3rd edn. Hampshire: Palgrave Macmillan.

Tierney, W.G. (1995) '(Re)Presentation and voice'. *Qualitative Inquiry*, 1, 379.

Tooley, J. and Darby, D. (1998) *Educational Research: A critique – a survey of published educational research*. London: Ofsted.

Toynton, R. (2006) 'Invisible other: Understanding safe spaces for queer learners and teachers in adult education'. *Studies in the Education of Adults*, 38 (2), 178–94.

Tyler, C. (2005) *Traveller Education: Accounts of good practice*. Stoke-on-Trent: Trentham Books.

UNICEF (2005) 'Fact sheet: A summary of the rights under the Convention on the Rights of the Child'. Online. www.unicef.org/crc/index_30228.html (accessed November 2010).

United Kingdom (2011) 'House of Lords. Parliamentary debates (official Hansard) c708'. Online. http://tinyurl.com/q8ahong (accessed July 2011).

— (2013) 'House of Commons. Parliamentary debates (official Hansard), c864'. Online. http://tinyurl.com/odctj8j (accessed March 2014).

Ureche, H. and Franks, M. (2007) *This Is Who We Are: A study of the views and identities of Roma, Gypsy and Traveller young people in England*. London: The Children's Society.

Van Galen, J.A. (1991) 'Ideologues and pedagogues: Parents who teach their children at home'. In Van Galen, J.A. and Pitman, M.A. (eds) *Home Schooling: Political, historical and pedagogical perspectives*. Norwood, NJ: Ablex, 63–76.

Villenas, S., Deyhle, D. and Parker, L. (1999) 'Critical Race Theory and praxis: Chicano(a) Latino(a) and Navajo struggles for dignity , educational equality and social justice'. In Parker, L., Deyhle, D. and Villenas, S., *Race Is … Race Isn't: Critical Race Theory and qualitative studies in education*. Oxford: Westview, 31–53.

Walker, R. (1985) *Applied Qualitative Research*. Aldershot: Gower.

Warrington, C. (2006) *Children's Voices: The views and experiences of young Gypsies and Travellers*. Ipswich: Ormiston Children and Families Trust.

Webb, S. (2010) *Elective Home Education in the UK*. Stoke-on-Trent: Trentham Books.

Webb, S. and Webb, B. (1932) *Methods of Social Study*. London: Longman, Green and Co.

Weiss, C. (ed.) (1977) *Using Social Research in Public Policy Making*. Farnborough: Saxon House.

Weiss, C. (1991) 'Policy research: Data, ideas, or arguments'. In Wagner, P., Weiss, C.H., Wittrock, B. and Wollman, H. (eds) *Social Sciences and Modern States: National experiences and theoretical crossroads*. Cambridge: Cambridge University Press, 307–32.

Wellington, J. (2000) *Educational Research: Contemporary issues and practical approaches*. London: Continuum.

Wilkin, A., Derrington, C. and Foster, B. (2009) *Improving the Outcomes for Gypsy, Roma and Traveller pupils: Literature review*. Research Report DCSF-RR077. London: DfE.

Wilkin, A., Derrington, C., White, R., Martin, K., Foster, B., Kinder, K. and Rutt, S. (2010) *Improving the Outcomes for Gypsy, Roma and Traveller pupils: Final report*. Research Report DFE-RR043. London: DfE.

Willers, M. (2012) 'Tackling inequalities suffered by Gypsies and Travellers'. *TAT News, Newsletter Spring 2012*, Travellers Advice Team.

Winstanley, C. (2009) 'Too cool for school? Gifted children and homeschooling'. *Theory and Research in Education*, 7 (3), 347–62.

Wyer, D., Danaher, P., Kindt. I. and Moriarty, B. (1997) 'Interactions with Queensland show children: Enhancing knowledge of educational contexts'. *Queensland Journal of Educational Research*, 13, 28–40.

Wyness, M. (20012) *Childhood and Society*, 2nd edn. London: Palgrave MacMillan.

Yosso, T.J. (2006) 'Whose culture has capital? A Critical Race Theory discussion of community cultural wealth'. In Dixson, A.D. and Rousseau, C.K. (eds), *Critical Race Theory in Education: All God's children got a song*. Oxford: Routledge, 167–91.

Zamudio, M.M., Russell, C., Rios, A.F. and Bridgeman, J.L. (2011) *Critical Race Theory Matters: Education and ideology*. New York: Routledge.

Index